ISLAND OF DREAMS

Dan Boothby

ISLAND OF DREAMS

A Personal History of a Remarkable Place

PICADOR

First published 2015 by Picador
an imprint of Pan Macmillan
20 New Wharf Road, London N1 9RR
Associated companies throughout the world
www.panmacmillan.com

ISBN 978-1-5098-0075-9

Excerpts from this book first appeared, in a slightly different form,
in 'The Island Review' (www.theislandreview.com) and in
'An Antidote to Indifference', Issue 9 (Caught by the River, 2014).

The extract from Gavin Maxwell's letter to Donald Mitchell on page 251 is reproduced
by permission of Gavin Maxwell Enterprises Ltd.

Photograph of Kyleakin Lighthouse Island on page v © iStock.com/fotoVoyager.

1 3 5 7 9 8 6 4 2

A CIP catalogue record for this book is available from the British Library.

Map artwork by Hemesh Alles
Printed and bound by CPI Group (UK) Ltd, Croydon, CR0 4YY

Visit **www.picador.com** to read more about all our books
and to buy them. You will also find features, author interviews and
news of any author events, and you can sign up for e-newsletters
so that you're always first to hear about our new releases.

Kyleakin Lighthouse Island

FOR MY FAMILY

and *in memoriam*

OLWEN DAFYDD

(1968–2014)

First Skyeman, at bar, in August: 'Aye, Donald, it's been
   raining since July.'
Second Skyeman, after deep thought: 'Just so, just so.
   Which July?'

> From *Hamish's Mountain Walk*, 1978
> (with apologies to Hamish Brown)

O come wi' me where the sea-birds fly
Remote and far by the Isle of Skye –
Away wi' the winds a-sailing!
Where dreams are the gifts availing –

From 'Come with Me', Pittendrigh MacGillivray, 1923

Prosecuting Counsel: 'Do you wish to comment on the
   statement you have signed?'
The Fool [hanging by his foot from a rope]: 'All is true,
   milord, as remembered.'

> From *Truth or Consequences*, P. F. Standhope, 1914

It was the poet Cowper who said that God made the country and man made the town, and no more appropriate words were ever written; for the country at all seasons of the year is like a big fascinating storybook, with no two pages alike – a book so large, that you can go on reading and turning over the pages every day of your life, and the deeper you get into it, the more beautiful and wonderful it becomes.

From *Wild Nature Wooed and Won*, Pike and Tuck, 1909

Contents

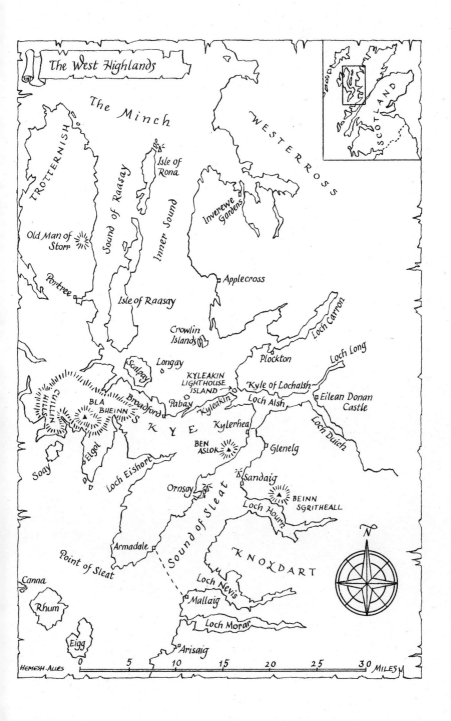

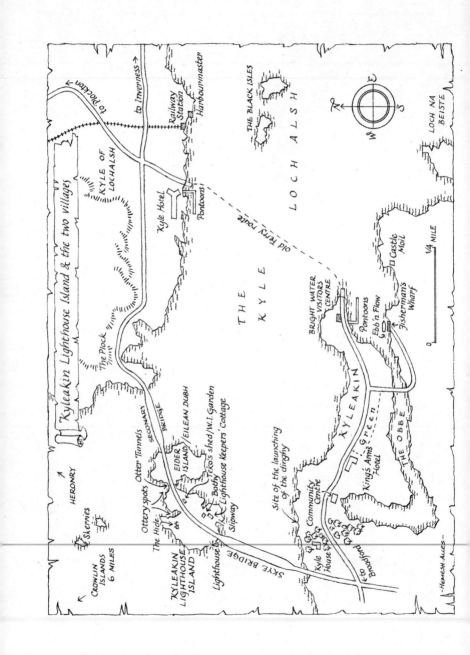

Kyleakin Lighthouse Island & the two villages

to Plockton
to Inverness →
Railway Station
Harbourmaster
THE BLACK ISLES
LOCH NA BEISTE
N
E
S
W
LOCH ALSH
KYLE OF LOCHALSH
Kyle Hotel
Pontoons
old ferry route
THE KYLE
BRIGHT WATER VISITORS CENTRE
Pontoons
Ebb'n Flow
Castle Moil
Fisherman's Wharf
¼ MILE
0
The Plock
HERONRY
Skerries
CROWLIN ISLANDS 6 MILES
Otter Tunnels
EIDER ISLAND / EILEAN DUBH
Bothy
kos shed / W.I. Garden
Lighthouse Keepers Cottage
Slipway
The Hide
Ottery spots
SECONARY BRIDGE
KYLEAKIN LIGHTHOUSE ISLAND
Lighthouse
SKYE BRIDGE
Site of the launching of the dinghy
KYLEAKIN
Green
THE OBBE
Community Centre
King's Arms Hotel
Kyle House
to Broadford
— HAMISH ALES —

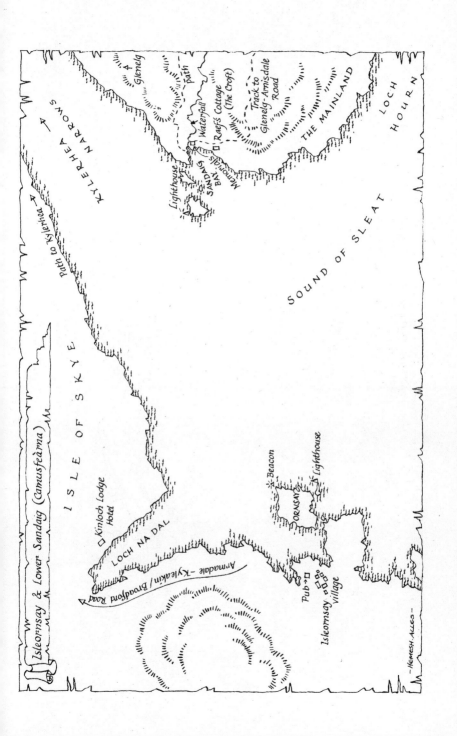

Isleornsay & Lower Sandaig (Camusfeàrna)

KYLERHEA

Path to Kylerhea →

ISLE OF SKYE

Glenelg

Path

Waterfall

Rae's Cottage (The Croft)

Lighthouse

SANDAIG BAY

Memorial Stone

Track to Glenelg-Arnisdale Road

THE MAINLAND

LOCH HOURN

SOUND OF SLEAT

Kinloch Lodge Hotel

LOCH NA DAL

Armadale-Kyleakin/Broadford Road →

Beacon

Lighthouse

ORNSAY

Pub →

Isleornsay village

—HENESH·ACES—

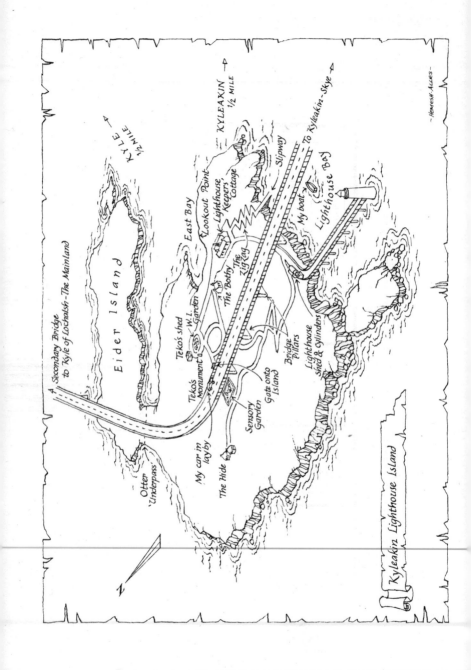

Kyleakin Lighthouse Island

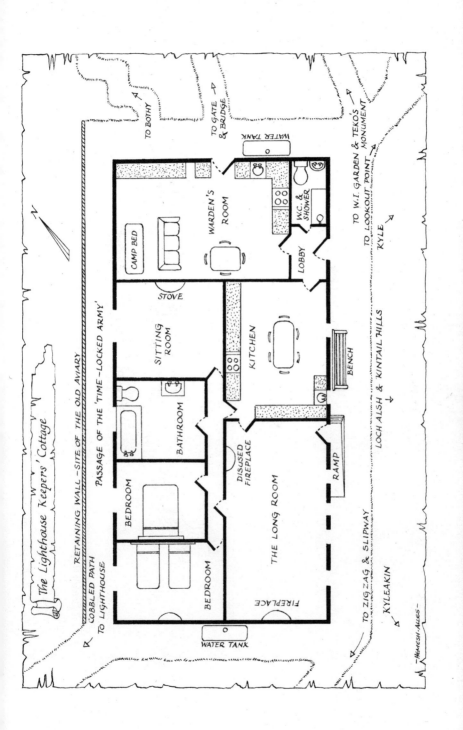

The Lighthouse Keepers' Cottage

RETAINING WALL – SITE OF THE OLD AVIARY

COBBLED PATH

PASSAGE OF THE 'TIME-LOCKED ARMY'

TO LIGHTHOUSE

TO BOTHY

TO GATE & BRIDGE

WATER TANK

WARDEN'S ROOM

W.C. & SHOWER

LOBBY

TO W.I. GARDEN & TEKO'S MONUMENT

TO LOOKOUT POINT MONUMENT

KYLE

CAMP BED

STOVE

SITTING ROOM

KITCHEN

BENCH

BATHROOM

DISUSED FIREPLACE

THE LONG ROOM

RAMP

LOCH ALSH & KINTAIL HILLS

BEDROOM

BEDROOM

FIREPLACE

WATER TANK

TO ZIG ZAG & SLIPWAY

KYLEAKIN

– HEMESH ALLES –

Prologue

THE DREAMER

When I was fifteen years old, on a half-term break from boarding school, I came across a book, mis-shelved in the natural history section of the local library, entitled *Raven Seek Thy Brother*.

Perhaps it was the 'Raven' in the title that prompted me to pull down the book. I admired ravens and the rest of the crow family, although I had reservations about the magpie, for it is an opportunist thief and a cad. But on the whole, corvids are the brightest, longest-lived and most inquisitive of all British birds. Even the ugliest – the rook, with its baggy trousers and crone's nose – has a certain raggedy-arsed charm.

The spine of the book was black gloss, with the title, publisher and author's name picked out in bold white capitals. It caught the eye. On the front cover, the author's name and the title – also in bold white capitals on black – topped and tailed an illustration of a white house with a slate-grey roof standing in isolation in a field of rough grass. The window frames and front door were a pale Mediterranean blue. A rosebush climbed up the front of the house, a low wooden fence encircled it. There was a small lean-to shed. Tools had been left lying on the grass. There was a ladder, a water butt, a wooden garden gate. The door of the house was ajar.

Behind the house were mountains, sheep grazing, a rocky outcrop on a sandy beach, a patch of sea. The sky was a menacing grey, but amidst the murk was a sliver of pale blue and there, in that shard of brightness above the lonely house, a raven flew.

I opened the book and flicked through its pages. It had been published in 1968 – some sixteen years before I found it – and was the last in a trilogy about the house and its environs, which the author called Camusfeàrna, the Gaelic for 'the Bay of Alders'. The house, an old lighthouse keepers' cottage, stood on the extreme edge of the western seaboard of the Highlands of Scotland and apart from a small 'but 'n' ben' cottage adjacent, the nearest habitation was a mile and a half away over a hill. Close-by, and just offshore, was a mini archipelago. Black and white photographs accompanied the text: a sitting room cluttered with books and pictures and otters, creels hanging from the ceiling and tins of food stacked on shelves like Scott's hut in the Antarctic; the surrounding hills, a broken-down Willys jeep on the track above the house; lighthouses and islands backed by snow-capped mountains; boats and dogs;

Icelandic ponies and whaling stations and frozen waterfalls; photographs of boys the same age as I was, playing
with otters.

The endpapers were pen-and-ink sketches of an otter
swimming, turning somersaults, flowing. The inside flap
of the dust jacket had a short biography of the author,
Gavin Maxwell, and a photograph of him – a middle-
aged man, asleep in a rickety armchair with an otter on his
lap.

I closed the book and caressed its glossy cover as I
continued my tour of the library, trawling for other books
– other worlds – to escape into. My brother, sisters and I
had been brought up to all intents and purposes fatherless,
and for the first four years of my life we had lived with our

mother in a gypsy caravan by the side of various roads. Eventually we had moved on to a commune in Norfolk and then a series of isolated houses surrounded by flat arable farmland and potholed tracks. I was growing up with most of my mind sunk into books and, at fifteen, although I had no idea of what I wanted to be, I devoured books about travelling the world, sailing in small boats, living in out-of-the-way places, natural history, and writers' lives. I read few novels; I was after facts. But at that age, among much else, I had yet to discover that all writing, even non-fiction and autobiography, is a blend of the blandly real and well-judged lies.

≈

After reading *Raven Seek Thy Brother* over a night and a day, I asked my family and friends if they knew anything about Gavin Maxwell. They had heard of *Ring of Bright Water*, his first book about his Highland home, but knew nothing else about the man. Scotland had never been on our map as a holiday destination – it was too distant and too hilly for trips out with the horse and wagon. In those days, which seem so far away now, before internet search engines and online encyclopaedias, there were no quick answers and a researcher had only the library, the telephone and the letter. I went back to school when half-term ended and in the school library found *The Otters' Tale* – a book Maxwell had put together for children in 1962. It is a large-format book, an abridgement of, and in parts an expansion on, *Ring of Bright Water*, and it contains a great many photographs: mainly of the otters Mij, Edal and Teko, but also of Camusfeàrna, of Maxwell himself, and of the boys Jimmy Watt and Terry Nutkins, who had lived with Maxwell and looked after the otters. I went through the photographs in *The Otters' Tale* time and again, scrutinizing the backgrounds with a magnifying glass to see what extra details I could glean from them.

Later that year flu swept through the classrooms and dormitories of my school, and I found myself washed up on the languid atoll of the school sickbay. Away from the grind of boarding-school life, my fellow refugees and I lazed in our beds while nurses in blue pinafores came round at intervals to dole out paracetamol and orange juice and meals on trays. And in the sickbay bookcase I discovered a copy of *Ring of Bright Water*, which I rush-read before being cast back into the surf of school. Lyrical and jocular, *Ring of Bright Water* is for the most part a bright, light book about beginnings, but it didn't resonate with my teenage self as *Raven Seek Thy Brother* had. *Raven Seek Thy Brother* is an altogether darker book – about the end of a dream. Maxwell called it a true sequel to *Ring of Bright Water*, and in it he ascribed blame to a curse laid upon a rowan tree at Camusfeàrna for turning everything sour.

When school ended, I bought with my pocket money a paperback of *The Rocks Remain*, the second of the

Camusfeàrna trilogy, in which Maxwell continued the story of life at Camusfeàrna, though much of the book is taken up with Maxwell's travels, his marriage, and his winter sojourns abroad.

Reading about Maxwell's adventures, I hankered after the life he described in the books: the romance of mountain, sea and rock, vivid colour and violent sky. The remoteness and beauty of Camusfeàrna evoked a yearning in me, so opposite was it from the flat, tamed, featureless and often muddy land where I lived. A shy, solitary child, my dreaming head was always stuck in a story, where I'd meet interesting characters – or characters I thought to be more like me than the people around me; where I had company, where life made sense and all the strands tied up neatly in the end. And I was a 'commune kid'. We weren't exactly legion. There was a stigma attached to being brought up different, laid on us by 'the straights' – normal people. I had a choice: accept my status and brazen it out, or retreat from those that might hurt me. I'd watched my brother get bruised at his school for taking the first option and so I chose the latter, and retreated into books.

I wanted to be in Gavin Maxwell's stories. I wanted the life I imagined those boys had. I wanted danger and adventure: to experience wild storms at sea and bouncing trips aboard rickety Land Rovers along rough mountain roads. I wanted to live in a house where otters and deerhounds stretched out to sleep by the fire and where erudite, sophisticated house guests came visiting from abroad. I wanted it all but could only get it in books. And so I read, and dreamed, and projected; for the present was merely to be endured, until life could become more exciting.

Raven Seek Thy Brother is a brooding book, full of self-pity, foreboding and loss; a requiem to a lost idyll; and it grabbed me and haunted me and pulled me headlong into obsession: with the man who wrote it and the world he so powerfully described. In its epilogue Maxwell wrote, 'In the small hours of 20 January 1968, fire swept through Camusfeàrna, gutting the house and destroying everything that was in it.' One of his otters, Edal, died in the fire, Maxwell lost practically everything he owned, and shortly afterwards he moved to the cottage on Kyleakin Lighthouse Island. In the other books about his Highland home, Maxwell had made a good job of disguising the location of Camusfeàrna, but after the fire, when it couldn't matter any more, he told us where it was. In the foreword to *Raven Seek Thy Brother*, he wrote:

> With the necessarily precise placing of the two lighthouses of Ornsay and Kyleakin it will be obvious to any interested reader that Camusfeàrna is Sandaig, by Sandaig Lighthouse, on the mainland of Scotland some five miles south of Glenelg village.

I got out the family atlas and tracked down Glenelg, Sandaig, and the lighthouse islands of Ornsay and

Kyleakin, and that summer of 1985 – the summer of Live Aid – in a house surrounded by flat fields, I dreamt up a journey to mountains.

One

SUMMER DAZE, 2005

You drive up from the South and reach Glasgow and think you're near but you're not even close. You drive on, through the shabby-grand, second-city streets and out into a landscape untamed and open. You edge the car around Loch Lomond – skirting those bonnie banks – and catch flashes of quicksilver and blue through fir trees and crash barriers and over low stone walls. On, on, four hours of gunning the engine further on; over Rannoch Moor and down through haunted Glen Coe, past the lump of Ben Nevis (if you are lucky and it's a fine cloudless day) and through Fort William; over the Spean River and the Caledonian Canal, past the Cluanie Inn and the Five Sisters of Kintail, until by Eilean Donan Castle in Dornie you glimpse it. There, at last, at the mouth of Loch Alsh, sitting beneath the sleek, grey stretch of the Skye Bridge. The tiny lighthouse island. The windows of the cottage wink, the Cuillin Mountains rise massive and disinterested behind. Another forty minutes and you'll be home. You swing the car around the end of the loch and on down the hill into Kyle. Only half a mile to go now, past the railway station, past the slipway where the Skye ferries used to dock, past the old tollbooth and up the incline of the approach road. You slow, pull into the lay-by beside the gate in the otter-wall and switch off the engine. Because you've arrived.

To an American or anyone from a 'big country' the distances involved would appear minuscule, but to a Briton, who believes his country to be of a manageable size, seven hundred miles is a very long way indeed. I had driven for fourteen hours and by the time I was on the final furlong up onto the Skye Bridge my car was coughing and kicking like a sick horse. I was amazed, frankly, that the car, bought for less than a song from a ferret of a man in a pub in West Wales ('I've found just the thing you're looking for, mate. I'll fix it up for you'), had made it at all. I got out of the car and the damp clean odour of the Highlands and the silence hit me like a dose of salts. It was already late on this June summer evening but this far north the sky was still bright. I walked, stiff from the extreme drive, up onto the span of the bridge to look down on my new home. I was above the island up there, above even the lighthouse; a speck of humanity thirty metres above the sea. To the south-east lay Loch Alsh and the two villages – Kyle of Lochalsh on the mainland and Kyleakin on the

Isle of Skye. Behind me and to the north-west, the Inner Sound led out to the open sea.

I'd been mailed a set of keys, a hand-drawn map of the island, and instructions. I slotted a key into the lock on the gate, bumped my shoulder to rain-swollen wood and lurched through onto a pathway of pale grit. A rowan – the witches' tree of the Hebrides, its berries still green – loitered nearby. I squeaked the gate shut and crunched to a crossroads where another rowan – this one dead and rotting – clutched a crow's nest leaking wisps of wool. The massive bulk of the Skye Bridge leered over the island behind me like a bramble tendril, one end rooted on the mainland, the other on Skye. I walked on past a small stone building standing on a honeysuckle-strewn bluff and came to the lighthouse cottage.

I tried another of the keys in a half-windowed door in the gable end and found myself in a room that smelt of mould and long disuse. There was a wardrobe, a sofa-bed, a TV on a chest of drawers, a table and an armchair. A galley kitchen. A seven-foot-high fridge-freezer towered in a corner. Everything in the room had seen better days. The floor had been raised and there was a step down by a door-way onto a square of the original stone floor, patterned with sweat stains from rising damp. The door opened to a lobby and a shower cubicle. Coats and knitted scarves and a hi-vis puffer jacket hung on pegs in the lobby above a pair of paint-spattered yellow sea boots and a chaos of cleaning equipment. A poster of an otter was pinned to one of the off-white walls. Another door opened to the front of the cottage. Like a house-sitter, I had that sweet desire to peer and pry and poke around, but the door to the rest of the house was locked and I hadn't been given the key.

The fridge-freezer in my room clicked and began to hum loudly. I went back into the room where I would be living and looked through the half-windowed door to the path and the brown and grey mountains beyond and for the first time in my life felt what it must be like: that heady rush of home-ownership.

The sun was setting as I strolled with a very light step back up the path to the car. The western sky over the Inner Sound was aflame and a rusty cloud shaped like an angel was heading north on light airs. I ferried my belongings to my room, then went to sit on a rain-warped bench at the front of the cottage to take in the view. The summer solstice – the longest day of the year – was a week behind me and all around me was everything I'd dreamed of: mountains, boats, islands, the sea, and Gavin Maxwell's old haunts. I was entering the myth that had gripped me all those years ago as a boy.

≈

The beginning of the Maxwell myth goes like this:

A man in his forties, a writer, a painter, a naturalist – a

poet – spends part of each year living in a remote lighthouse keepers' cottage on the western seaboard of the Scottish Highlands. 'Camusfeàrna', he calls this place, and he has been coming here since he was first offered the lonely house on its isolated promontory after the Second World War by an old friend from university days. The nearest village is five miles away, by rough footpath up mountainside and down unmetalled road, though it is a little closer by sea. The writer retreats to the house, alone but for his beloved dog, Jonnie, to write and to explore the wild surrounding land and sea where life is harsh and elemental. Then Jonnie dies, leaving the writer feeling bereft and doubly alone. He grieves, and casts around for another companion to keep him company in his solitude – an animal – for other humans, with their complications and demands, have only ever brought the man sadness.

He has a book to write, and in 1956 accompanies Wilfred Thesiger – that craggy-faced, hard-as-nails explorer of the Arabian Sands – to the marshlands of Southern Iraq to gather material for what will become *A Reed Shaken by the Wind*. Some of the Marsh Arabs keep otters as pets and, during his last days in Iraq, the writer is handed an otter cub. He takes the cub with him to London, where he keeps a studio flat. The cub, Mijbil, grows and proves to be an amusing, intelligent and loving pet, though always fiercely independent, always part wild, and too boisterous for the cramped London flat. The writer – charmed, and no longer lonely – takes the otter to his Highland home, where Mijbil delights in the surroundings, swimming free in the burn and the sea. And the writer delights in the antics of Mij – a wild creature that has accepted him as its friend and holds so much more fascination than a faithful, obedient dog. Mij is unique, and what's more he is of a subspecies of otter previously unknown to science. Mijbil's genus is named by the scientific community after the man who discovered it. *Lutrogale perspicillata maxwelli*: 'Maxwell's Otter'.

Idylls are merely episodes. Mij is a constant distraction. The writer must work and travel. He asks a friend, the poet Kathleen Raine, to look after Mij at Camusfeàrna while he returns to London and the writing desk. Raine is as enamoured of the Highlands and as charmed by Mij as the writer. And Raine harbours a deep love for the writer. To be allowed into the sanctity of his home, for her, is a balm. She writes poetry to him, she leaves love tokens for him to find, she loves the otter as she loves him.

But Mijbil wanders, as wild territorial animals tend to do. He roams further and further from Camusfeàrna and one day he disappears altogether. Raine searches frantically, fearfully, guiltily. For the writer had warned her, wild otters are considered vermin in the Highlands and are routinely killed by the crofters. Mij must wear a harness, always – to signal he is pet, not wild. But Raine had removed Mij's harness and Mij had strayed, too far, and was chopped with a spade by a road mender from the village.

The writer returns from his travels, forgives Raine (who for the rest of her life can never forgive herself), but is bereft. He casts around for another otter, for he has fallen in love with Mij's kind, and one day, sitting in the bar of a hotel in Kyle of Lochalsh, he spies a man and a woman walking an otter on a lead. He rushes from the bar to intercept the trio, gabbles. The couple, on holiday from a posting in Nigeria, are looking for a home for their pet otter, Edal. This is how fate works.

They agree to let the writer take Edal. Jimmy Watt, fifteen years old and having recently left school, is employed to look after Edal and to manage Camusfeàrna during the writer's absences. The summer of 1959 has come. There is an otter about the remote house once again and, almost unthinkingly, the man sits down at his desk one day and begins to write the story of Camusfeàrna. With lyrical precision he describes the wild seas and wide-open lands of the far North, so far away and so removed from the drab, clamorous cities of the South. And he tells of the life and death of Mij, and of his fateful finding of Edal; of otters, companions that have brought him so much joy.

Utopian literature was popular in the fifties and sixties. Books about wild places and living with wild animals were 'in'. T. H. White's *The Goshawk* had been published in 1951 and Michaela Denis's *Leopard in my Lap* appeared in 1954.

The Austrian ethologist Konrad Lorenz published *King Solomon's Ring* and *Man's Best Friend* in the mid-fifties and Gerald Durrell's classic *My Family and Other Animals* came out to acclaim in 1956. Rowena Farre's purely fictional 'autobiography', *Seal Morning*, about a Highland childhood and a trumpet-tooting pet seal, had been a huge best-seller in 1957, as had *The Hills is Lonely*, Lillian Beckwith's 1959 comic novel about the goings-on of a village on the edge of the Isle of Skye. Joy Adamson's Elsa-the-lioness book, *Born Free*, was on its way. There was something in the air.

Ring of Bright Water, charming, erudite, humorous and escapist, lavishly finished with photographs and drawings, was published in 1960 and instantly struck a chord. The book was a best-seller on both sides of the Atlantic, a UK Book Society non-fiction choice and an American Book of the Month Club choice. In its first year of publication 100,000 hardback copies were bought. (To date 2 million copies have been sold, and that doesn't include the myriad foreign-language editions.) *Ring of Bright Water* was number 10 in the American book industry's *Publishers Weekly* list of best-selling books of 1960. What Maxwell achieved with that book (his fifth) is a writer's dream. He became rich, and famous. But . . .

≈

Towards the end of October 2004, seeking shelter from a grizzly afternoon of West Highland rain, I had looked in on the Bright Water Visitors' Centre in Kyleakin. After I'd pushed open the door and shaken some of the rain off me onto the doormat, a woman of about fifty, with a drawn, pinched face had come through a doorway at the back of the room and bustled about behind a mock-driftwood counter. I squelched around the overheated and stuffy room, dripping warmed-up rain onto the polished pine floorboards. I was the only visitor. Double glazing on several of the picture windows had failed and condensation partially obscured the views of the harbour, the surrounding sea and the hills. Charts and posters and information boards lined the walls – how to tell a whale from a dolphin, dates and locations of recent wildlife sightings, a spotter's guide to seabirds, how to take part in RSPB surveys . . . A raised sandpit contained painted wooden animals and model fishing boats. There was a large plywood cut-out of the lighthouse, and photographs. Silent footage of an otter with cubs gambolling among rocks and seaweed played on a loop on a TV. I stuck my hand into holes in wall-mounted wooden cubes and felt a plastic crab, a rubber starfish, dried seaweed and sea shells. A corner of the room was devoted to Gavin Maxwell – a desk with a fan of his headed notepaper laid under glass, copies of his books, an album of photographs of Maxwell and the boys and the otters, of Camusfeàrna and the Lighthouse Island, and a facsimile of the handwritten first chapters of *Ring of Bright Water*. Part of the room was given over to the sale of toys and trinkets, souvenirs – the usual Highland-themed tat. 'Highland tunes' filled the silence. There was a strong smell of damp.

'How are the fortunes of the Trust?' I asked the worried-looking woman behind the counter that rain-drenched day. Susan Browning, the Director, had looked up and been eager to tell me her troubles. Funding had dried up, she said, visitor numbers were down, and income from the island tours and shop sales was meagre. The Trust's overdraft kept increasing. There hadn't been a resident warden on the island for two years. She worried about security. They were having to let the main accommodation of the lighthouse keepers' cottage to holidaymakers to bring in capital. They'd fitted a galley kitchen in the spare room in the cottage because they were thinking about advertising for a part-time warden/caretaker, but they couldn't really afford to pay a salary. She lay awake at night fretting about the future of the Centre and the Trust.

I listened, offered suggestions, agreed and wanted to help, both her and the Kyleakin Lighthouse Island Trust – for I knew all about the Trust. And I had visited the visitors' centre and the tiny 8.5 acre island several years before, in 2001, when it was all shiny brand new. But as always I was in transit, circling, en route to somewhere else, looking for but never finding the perfect place to land.

A week later I flew to India to sit out the northern winter and to work on a book I had provisionally entitled

Travels. It was to be about my life up to that point: about what it is to be a stray, to cast oneself adrift time and again from the pontoons of family, friends and a steady occupation, to see where one ends up. I had been drifting for more than twenty years by then, and I wasn't so sure it was such a fine and free thing to do any more.

One December day that winter, procrastinating, pondering my next move, surfing the internet, I googled 'Gavin Maxwell'. It was something I did periodically, to see if anything new came to light. Among the results was a link to the website of the Kyleakin Lighthouse Island Trust and it set me thinking. I went back to my typing and dreaming in Madras, and at the end of April 2005 returned to England with a completed first draft of my book. At the beginning of May I sent Susan Browning an email. Would the Trust like a volunteer to help out in the Bright Water Visitors' Centre or on the Lighthouse Island over the coming summer season? I wouldn't want paying, just a place to stay, free of charge if at all possible. Several days later I received a reply. More emails followed. Then, at the beginning of June, I got the news I'd been hoping for.

≈

The springs in the sofa bed in my room had been sprung some time way back in the annals of island history. Even if I hadn't been eager to get on with my new life, chances are I'd have hardly slept a wink. I was up by six the next morning – wide awake and eating breakfast outside on the bench. The sun was tracking over the Kintail hills, over the loch, across a clear blue sky. It was cold, but warming up nicely. A lawn, almost obliterated by a tangle of brambles and bracken, sloped steeply away from me down to a rocky shoreline and the loch. An alder tree stood at the loch's edge, its trunk obscured by more brambles and a mass of rosebay willowherb. Along the foreshore a hooded crow, with its sideways, skipping, Richard III gait, was jabbing at sea wrack and shells; foraging, casting aside.

Traffic was moving along the approach road between Kyle of Lochalsh and the bridge. Over in Kyle, a train was parked at the platform by the harbour. A helicopter rose up from a pile of brown industrial buildings, circled tightly over two small islands near the harbour and blattered towards me before bearing away over the bridge. Fishing boats were nodding at anchor in a nearby bay.

Half a mile away across the other side of the loch in Kyleakin, a shingle beach stretched below a strip-development of modern housing, a village green, a youth hostel and pubs. A tent, hidden from the road by a thicket of trees, had been pitched on grass above the beach. I sipped coffee and watched a woman crawl from the tent, scuttle into the trees, crouch for a moment and nimbly skip back in. Cars and vans were moving along the road behind the trees. A red-hulled fishing boat puttered around

Kyleakin slipway and motored past the island, leaving bubbles and Vs on calm water in its wake.

I had read how Maxwell had often sat where I was now sitting, a telescope planted on a table in front of him, spying on Kyle and Kyleakin. And, like him, I was to be cheered in my solitude by the sights and sounds, and by the companionship, of the villagers.

The Bright Water Visitors' Centre opened at ten on weekdays. I strolled over the bridge and took the road into Kyleakin. A gaggle of kids carrying fishing rods and pond-dipper nets approached, stomping along, practically running. One or two were on bikes. I stepped aside to let them pass. They swept by, gabbling excitedly, on a mission. I followed the road through the village to its end. Gulls floated above the yachts and the fishing boats tied to the pontoons in the marina behind the old ferry terminal.

An over-the-door cowbell tinkled as I opened the door to the Centre. Although the sun was shining strongly outside and I'd passed a number of tourists with cameras and awed faces, the Bright Water Visitors' Centre didn't seem to be attracting them. Susan Browning hovered behind the driftwood counter. The video footage of otters gambolling among rocks and seaweed played on the TV at the far end of the room. The dreadful 'Highland tunes' CD droned on.

I reintroduced myself to Susan – it'd been a few months – told her I'd settled in, and said thank you.

'Oh yes, I recognize you now,' Susan said, passing me a ream of timesheets. 'There are quite a few jobs that need doing on the island. Actually, I've made a list.'

She handed me another piece of paper.

'Sort out signage,' I read out, 'tidy up hide and bothy and interior of lighthouse, de-moss bothy steps, cut back brambles and pull up weeds from along edges of paths, plant gorse along wall on west side of island to stop trespassers, weed cobbled path, fix bench in front of house . . .'

'I'm sure there're other jobs you'll find need doing. Really, I'd like you to take the island on as your project. Are you any good at marketing? It would help such a lot if we could *really* put this place on the map and increase visitor numbers as a priority. Everyone loves Gavin Maxwell but how can they visit us if they don't know we're here?

'You should fill in the timesheets so that we can see what you've been doing. As we discussed over email, you work twenty hours a week in return for accommodation on the island. I'm afraid we can't pay you for any hours that you might put in over and above that. You said you could stay until the end of October? Pete Baggeley, one of the trustees, takes the tours at the moment, but hopefully that is something else you can help with. I'll be over on the island tomorrow lunchtime to get the cottage ready for the couple coming on Saturday.'

I walked back through Kyleakin clutching my timesheets and to-do list and stopped by the beach. The bridge loomed massive above me. Traffic passed along it, *kerr-lump, kerr-lump, kerr-lump*. A young woman opened the flap of the tent I'd spied from the island, skipped over pebbles in a swimsuit and dashed into the sea, flinging glittery droplets of water into the blue. She floated on her back for a moment, trod water and, on seeing me, waved. I waved back. She swept her arms back and forth through the water, spluttering and laughing.

'You should come in too,' she shivered. A German accent. 'It's freezing c-cold but very . . . life-giving.' I shook my head, waved again and tramped over the pebbles to the road. Up on the bridge, seagulls wheeled around me, sinking below the barriers, then with stiff wings riding the wind to soar high above.

Back on the island I looked for the young woman again, but she and her tent had gone.

≈

That afternoon, storing away my gear with all the doors of my room open, I heard the *whomp* of a door being slammed shut and footsteps approaching. A very casually dressed portly man in his sixties appeared at the doorway.

'I reckon the first job you could do is clear out the bothy,' he said. 'Pete, Pete Baggeley.'

I held out a hand and he gave me a funny look but shook it. 'I'm going up to meet the visitors for the tour. Coming?'

Pete slouched along, scuffing the heels of his wellington boots in the gravel as he went. He had an extremely lazy way of walking.

'Susan tells me you're a writer,' he said. 'You should fit in a treat up here. Skye's full of artists. Oh yes, we've got all kinds up here.' He snorted.

'I'm not really a writer,' I said. 'Not yet, anyway.'

'Not a Maxwell nut, are you? We get lots of those here, Maxwell nuts, otter nuts . . .'

'No,' I said.

I didn't think of myself as a 'nut'.

'You've been to Sandaig, or "Camusfeàrna" as some of them call it, I suppose.'

'I used to camp down there.'

'I've never met any of them. Terry Nutkins and Jimmy Watt and the rest of them. A lot of the stuff in the Long Room came from Jimmy. I heard Terry's got *eight* kids or something. Amazing.'

Heads were bobbing about on the other side of the gate, faces peering anxiously over the wall.

'At least we have the sun today,' Pete called out. He opened the gate and five warmly dressed people trundled through it to stand by the rowan tree. Pete launched into a spiel about the Kyleakin Island Trust and then led us around the island, all the while regaling us with stories about Maxwell, about lighthouse-keeping, about Highland life; laughing his easy, see-sawing, guffawing, slightly nervous, cynical tic of a laugh. I brought up the rear of our little group, listening to Pete and taking mental notes, but mostly taking in the changes that had occurred since I had last visited the island four years before.

The paths were no longer marble white, but grey, weed-ridden, mossy and thinly surfaced, much of the gravel having been washed away by the rain. The planks of wood used to edge the paths were submerged by thick clumps of vegetation, and rotten. The cobbled path between the lighthouse and the cottage was almost indiscernible beneath a blanket of moss and weeds; tentacles of prickly gorse spread along the few patches of grass that surrounded the house; the slipway was covered in seaweed and slime. I could see cracks in the cement on the lighthouse tower, and the wrought-iron gangway was rust-streaked and in need of repair. The exteriors of the cottage, bothy and lighthouse shed were a dirty white, the paintwork faded and damp-stained and flaking. Only the hide, a relatively new building, seemed in a good state. When Pete unlocked the door to the Long Room – a forty-foot room at the front of the house, which contained a number of Maxwell's belongings and served as a museum celebrating his life and work – there was a smell of damp and something rotting. The whole island looked uncared for, Nature swiftly reclaiming her own. We didn't see any otters.

'It will be good to have someone living on the island

again,' Pete said as we waved the disappointed otter-botherers off at the gate. 'There's been no one living here since Gregory left. There were a couple of part-time wardens a couple of years ago but nobody since.'

≈

I'd visited in the spring of 2001. It had been a hot day. I bought a ticket at the Centre and was taken across to the island in a little motorboat. There was no visitor access from the bridge back then. A bespectacled man of about my age, with short blond hair, wearing a hi-vis puffer jacket and paint-spattered yellow sea boots, a pair of binoculars dangling around his neck, met me off the boat. Gregory showed me around: the remains of the boatshed, the light-house, Teko's memorial, rockeries planted with aromatic shrubs and flowers (the Sensory and WI Gardens), the Long Room. We stood in the hide gazing out over the Inner Sound, and Gregory told me the names of the islands we could see in the sun. Huge cumulous clouds were drifting over Raasay, dappling the hills with sunlight and shade. I was the only visitor that day.

'You get used to beauty,' Gregory said. 'And the rain. You stop seeing it after a while.'

He asked me what I knew about Gavin Maxwell.

'A little,' I said. *More than you.*

Then he left me to wander about the island until the motorboat returned to take me back to Kyleakin, and I thought, *You've got my job, Gregory. You've got my job and you're living in my house.*

But thoughts and ideas flow through the mind and on in cascades, forever being submerged by the onslaught of more. I travelled away from the island that day and moved on to other things.

≈

'The start-up money ran out,' Pete was saying. 'When there was nothing left for proper salaries, the wardens skedaddled. We're all volunteers now, except Susan.'

The scent of honeysuckle hung in the air. I followed Pete into the bothy.

'So, do you think you can do it? Help out with the tours? There's a script Gregory wrote somewhere.' Pete rooted around in a filing cabinet, handed me a pamphlet.

'"Kyleakin Lighthouse Island: A Short History". That should give you a good grounding.' He pulled out a few pages of typescript from the filing cabinet. 'This is the script for the tours. If you could start taking a few from next week it'd be a great help. They break up my day.'

We meandered back up the path to his car.

'Looks in worse condition than mine,' I said.

'I call it the Silver Dream Machine.'

'But it isn't silver.'

'No,' Pete said as he started the engine and revved like mad. 'You'll find the island grabs you,' he said, raising his voice as he revved. 'I used to work clearing the paths; then I started doing the tours. You end up becoming fixated on the place. I want to step back from it. See you tomorrow, if there's a tour.'

He roared off, black smoke billowing out behind his jalopy as it farted up over the bridge and down into Kyleakin.

I sat at a desk in the bothy with the door open. A sparrow-sized bird – a whitethroat – was hopping about, perking in the brambles outside. It sang. The pamphlet Pete had given me was short, twelve pages, published by a local printing press in 1982. There were photographs of the lighthouse, of small boats moored in the bay at the front of the house, a photograph of Maxwell sitting on a bench in front of the cottage looking shifty in the dark glasses he habitually wore towards the end of his life.

I had trouble concentrating on the text. I leafed through Gregory's script and then looked at Susan Browning's to-do list and couldn't decide which of the jobs to tackle first. I wondered if instead I should start working my way through the filing cabinet, or tidy the bothy as Pete had suggested, or go for a walk around the island, or drive over to Skye, or go down the pub. I stared out of the window at the two villages, the surrounding islands and the mountains and sea. A strange feeling was coming over me, and it took me a moment or two to recognize it for what it was. I'd only experienced it once before, in Damascus. A new lover had gone away for the day and left me alone in her apartment. I hadn't known what the feeling was back then and had got frightened, had wondered if I wasn't going a little insane. For it *is* a kind of insanity, falling in love.

That evening, before bed, feeling calmer, I took a stroll around the island, looking for signs of otter. In the last of the twilight I stood stock-still by the wall of the cobbled path and waited, watching the water in the bay by the lighthouse. The traffic overhead had quietened for the night. The navigation lights on the bridge winked high above me. I waited and watched, but nothing stirred in the darkening sea before me.

≈

The following day, kitted out with gardening gloves and a trowel, I made a start on the to-do list. All morning I was bent down on one knee or the other, loosening and pulling out great hanks of grass and assorted weeds along the edges of the paths that criss-crossed the island. Devil's coach horses raised their abdomens and snapped their pincers at me as I shuffled along, prodding and pulling, turfing out beetles and ants and leatherjackets from their homes. Kneeling there, my eyes lowered to the level of a small boy's, the ground and all its minuscule life forms so much closer, I felt for the first time in years a sense of purpose. I was needed and had a role, something to take me away from myself. I was 'the Warden' and I would care for the island after its long neglect and I would love it and repair it and bring it to life again.

'I'm glad you're getting on with it.' Susan Browning's unsmiling sunglasses-covered face looked down at me. Her shoulders were up, her arms filled with clean, ironed linen.

'There's a car parked in the lay-by. They shouldn't park there. It's only meant for people staying on the island.'

'It's mine,' I said. 'The blue estate.'

'No, no. There's another one. These people park there so they can walk onto the bridge to look at the view and take photos but they shouldn't. I've phoned the Highland Council so many times to put up a No Parking sign but they never do anything.'

I stood up and mopped my brow. 'I'm sure they'll be gone soon,' I said. 'They're not doing any harm. It *is* a lay-by.'

Susan Browning tutted. 'Anyway, I suppose I better get on with the cleaning. I've arranged cover at the visitors' centre for a few hours but I must get back. There's so much needs doing all the time.'

'Can I help?' I said.

'It's better if I get on alone. It would only slow me down having help.' She trotted down the path to the cottage.

A little later I went to my room for a glass of water. Susan Browning was banging and crashing about in the cottage kitchen. I stepped through to the lobby, peered around the kitchen door.

'I wonder if I might see the rest of the house?'

'Go right ahead. Don't—! Oh good, you've taken those boots off.' She grabbed a vacuum cleaner and hauled it through a door into the house.

From the exterior, the lighthouse keepers' cottage looked like two long, back-to-back single-storey houses, and originally the cottage *had* been two dwellings – one for the Principal lighthouse keeper and his family, another for the Assistant keeper. Gavin Maxwell had had the dividing wall knocked down in order to create a single three-bedroomed house. Today, the bathroom, bedrooms and a small sitting room are situated off a dark corridor at the back of the house, their windows looking out to an alleyway and a patch of scrub beneath a high, curved wall of rock. Both Maxwell and his friend Richard Frere wrote about this alleyway. Ghosts are said to parade and chatter there. Frere heard them, visitors to the island have seen them. The Long Room had been the sitting room in Maxwell's day. My room – the former coal shed and work-shop – stretched across the north-west gable end of the cottage. Apart from my room and the Long Room, the rest of the house smelt of furniture polish and stately homes.

I found Susan Browning busily vacuuming the small sitting room at the back of the house. When I stuck my head around the door she switched off the machine.

'The Raffertys will be here sometime on Saturday. We tell people to arrive after 2 p.m. so we can get the cottage cleaned if there's been someone in the week before, but you never know with people *when* they're going to turn up. If I give you a set of keys could you meet the Raffertys when they arrive and give it to them? It's just that it's a fifty-mile round trip for me otherwise.'

I told her it wouldn't be a problem.

'Oh, that's wonderful,' she said and went back to her hoovering.

Later I found her sitting on the bench at the front of the house, a packed lunch spread out neatly beside her, a pair of binoculars in her lap.

'I've just *got* to eat something,' she said.

I stepped over the gravel in my socks and perched on the bench beside her. A bird feeder hung from a length of dowelling stuck in the slope of the lawn in front of us. A flock of greenfinches flitted between the feeder and the silver skeleton of a very dead tree.

'You've met Pete,' she said when she'd stopped chewing. 'Do you think you'll be able to help with the tours? There's a script somewhere.'

'Yes, I've read it,' I said.

'Pete always begins his tours in the Long Room but I like to leave that as the finale when I have to do the tours. It's better that way, I think, especially when Maxwell fans are on the tour.'

She started, raised the binoculars to her eyes.

'Is that an otter? Out in the bay there?' She waggled a finger in front of her.

The tide was ebbing, exposing sandbars and seaweed. Tangles of bladderwrack and kelp fronds floated lazily in the sun. We sat watching where she'd pointed. A herring gull flew down and settled on a sandbank.

'No. Just seaweed.' She sighed, and took another bite of her sandwich.

'I'm hoping to get Jimmy Watt over here in the next few weeks so we can go through the inventory of the artefacts in the Long Room together. We need to know what belongs to him and what belongs to the Trust. I know he donated some things at the beginning.'

'Have you met him?' I asked.

'Oh yes, several times. I get him to do my paintings. He's a picture-framer, you know. Lovely house, he has. A lovely man.' She sighed again.

'What do you paint?' I asked.

'Animals and birds. And I also paint rocks I find on the beach where we live. I enjoy it. I'm trying to sell some at the moment but nobody's buying.' She sighed again. 'There's a craft exhibition in Portree in a few weeks and I'm desperately trying to get a collection ready for that.' She twisted the cap off a bottle of water and drank.

A loud grunting came from the bay in front of the house. We looked at each other.

'Quietly,' Susan Browning shushed. We waded through bracken and heather to the edge of the lawn.

A seal the size of a cow was basking on one of the flatter rocks at the sea's edge. Another, smaller, seal was attempting to haul itself out next to it. The larger seal was grouching at the smaller seal, galumphing and flipper-waving and groaning. Susan Browning and I peered over the rocks.

'Such a *wonderful* thing to witness,' she whispered. 'We're so *lucky* living up here.'

'Like kids squabbling over toys,' I said. '"It's mine! No, mine! I found it first!"'

The smaller seal, out-manoeuvred by the sheer mass of the other, gave up and swam off. The heffalump, its point having been made, flopped into the sea and followed it.

We walked back to the bench.

'By the way, you should go and see Johnny Ach,' she said. 'He's been involved with the Trust from the beginning and was chairman until recently. He's the harbourmaster in Kyle and knows everything. After Gregory and the other wardens left he used to take the tours during his lunch break. Now we've got Pete, of course, and you.'

She placed the remains of her picnic into a Tupperware box and shut the lid with a snap.

≈

I asked Pete if he would accompany me on my first tour.

'You'll be fine. I imagine you know more about Maxwell and his crew than I do. Seen any otters yet?'

I shook my head.

'They're around. But I rarely see them on a tour. I often see them in the evenings down by the river when I'm out walking the dogs. Everybody thinks they're rare but they're everywhere up here.'

The Raffertys – an emphysemic couple from Glasgow – waddled and wheezed onto the island early on Saturday to stay the week. I welcomed them, handed them their keys and escaped to the bothy to read. Having strangers staying in the cottage, hearing their voices in the kitchen and coming across them on my wanderings around the island felt, back then, like an invasion. I wanted time alone with the island and its memories.

That afternoon I drove over the bridge to Skye and nursed my car the short distance up and down the hills to the Otter Haven at Kylerhea. I sat out of the rain in a hide overlooking the narrow stretch of sea between Skye and the mainland and scanned the shorelines and rocks and water for a small black head, a loping gait or a long flat tail. I saw plenty of seals and herons and gulls. I watched a fishing boat make slow progress against the tidal race, punching its way south into the Sound of Sleat. The Glenachulish turntable ferry plied back and forth across the Narrows. A Lilliputian lighthouse, which looked familiar but had not been there on my 2001 trip north, had been erected above the slipway on the Glenelg side. But I saw no otters. Nearby was the large white house, recently painted, the grounds neat and orderly, where Jimmy Watt lived. An estate car and a Land Rover were parked in the driveway. A small motor boat tied to a mooring buoy was bobbing in a nearby bay.

The wipers slashed across the windscreen as I drove back home. The road in front of me and the hills and sea blurred then cleared, blurred then cleared. Rain fell into the night and continued to fall for most of the following week.

≈

'You learn to work around the rain,' Pete said one day before a tour. 'When it's raining you do indoor things and when it stops you go outside again.'

I took tours. It was like taking the stage – daunting before you step out, invigorating once you're on and exhilarating or exhausting depending on the audience. I tidied up the Long Room, polished and dusted, and murdered moths daily.

I walked into Kyle to see Johnny Ach. Pete had told me that Johnny 'Ach' Macrae, of the Clan Macrae – whose traditional clan-lands we lived on – was considered by many to be the King of Kyle. He had been born down the road at Achmore (thus 'Ach' – to distinguish him from other local Johnnys) and had lived all his life in Kyle. And as far as the Kyleakin Island Trust went, Johnny Ach was the monarch, the rest mere parliamentarians – transient and ever-changing do-gooders.

I found the harbourmaster's office and tripped in. A number of burly men togged out in sea boots and wet-weather gear stood bantering in a large, carpeted office. A picture window gave a panoramic view over Kyle Harbour to the Black Islands, Kyleakin and Skye. None of the men looked at me when I entered.

'I'm looking for Johnny Ach,' I said finally.

'Aye, that'll be me.' A large man leaning against a desk, dressed in jeans and a light blue shirt, the only man there not wearing sea boots, glanced over at me.

I told him who I was. 'I'm looking for a boat,' I said.

'Well, you've come to the right place,' said Johnny Ach brightly.

The loiterers wandered away.

'And a set of tide tables for the year.'

'Ah, well. We may be out of those. We're after getting some more run off on the photocopier. What will you be wanting a boat for?'

'For the island,' I said. 'For clearing rubbish off the shoreline. And because an island needs a boat.'

'Leave it with me,' said Johnny.

'Right then,' I said and turned to go.

'Hang on,' Johnny said. 'I've been meaning to come over to see you.'

He had a confidence about him that any man might wish for, and intelligent, sparky blue eyes. I imagined his flushed, florid face to be a badge of honour, a reminder of all the whisky sessions in all the captain's cabins of all the ships that had ever sailed into Kyle.

'How are things on the island?' he asked.

'I'm clearing the paths and I want to paint the house and the bothy and lighthouse shed, and sort out the damp and the moth infestation in the Long Room. They've got into the carpets. And I'd like to open up the fireplace in there and get some warmth into the walls.'

'That's good,' said Johnny. 'Anything you need?'

'A boat,' I said, 'and a set of tide tables.'

'Ha.' Johnny looked out the window for a moment. 'Have you a minute?'

I followed him into a meeting room and sat at a table. He got me a cup of coffee, sat across from me and swung his boatshoe-shod feet onto the tabletop. He leaned back in his chair. We looked at each other.

'The Trust is in a bad way, I think,' I said.

'People left,' Johnny said, as if he'd been betrayed.

'And now there's no money. No income.'

'No,' he said, then took his feet off the table and sat up, 'I mean, aye . . . there will be. Match-funding!'

'?'

'You raise a little money from one source and then you go and talk to other sources and say, 'Look, we've already raised this amount from A because he knows our cause is worthwhile, can you match it?' Then once you have B onboard you set up a meeting with C, and on it goes. That's how it works.'

'But will it cover the Trust's debts?'

'Everybody has debts,' Johnny said and shrugged. 'Once we get funding in place again we'll get rid of the debts right enough.'

He knew people, influential people. Johnny Ach knew everybody. He sat on committees and councils and was fluent in form-filling officialese. He was one of *them*, but his first loyalty was to his community.

'Up here we do things the West Highland way. Always have, always will. It just takes time, that's all,' he said.

Unlike the parliamentarian trustees, Johnny Ach was in for the long haul. He saw a bigger picture and took the long view. Most people's plans so often sound like what they are: pipe dreams and gaseous pub talk. Johnny Ach spoke with such energy and force and intelligence that the realization of his plans sounded not only possible, but easily achievable. Money would come, there'd be salaries again, the boat trips across to the island from Kyleakin would resume, there'd be open-access days when the island would be open for everyone to visit for free; and what about turning the bothy into a cafe? It's a great location for one.

I could have sat for a long time listening to Johnny throwing ideas around. I'm sure many have.

At eleven o'clock that night it was still light, not quite light enough to read by, but almost. Up above the island, in a patch of muted blue between white-grey rags of cloud, I could see only one star, bright and twinkling.

≈

The Gaelic name for the Isle of Skye is *Eilean à Cheo*, which translates into English as 'the Misty Isle'. My dictionary defines an isle or an island as 'a mass of land that is surrounded by water and is smaller than a continent'. The Isle of Skye and Kyleakin Lighthouse Island, then, remain islands, though with the coming of the Skye Bridge that status has been diminished, connected to the mainland as they are by concrete and steel. But before the opening of the bridge they were proper islands and to visit meant taking a boat. It was an event.

Ferries had plied the Kyle–Kyleakin route since the 1600s, but by the end of the twentieth century the popularity of the route had led to mile-long queues through the villages. Coachloads of tourists, and lorries and traffic of all kinds, slowed the turnaround rate. Nurses and postmen and tradespeople had trouble getting to work. Locals and tourists alike were left waiting, sometimes for hours. The ferries simply couldn't cope. Something had to change.

A consortium of investors put up £25 million. (The final cost would approach £39 million.) Land in Kyleakin and Kyle, and the Kyleakin Lighthouse Island, was bought by compulsory purchase order. Construction of the Skye Bridge began in 1992. Three years of rock-blasting, bulldozing and splashing about of concrete followed. Navigation lights were placed on the bridge and the lighthouse was decommissioned. The ferries continued to run until the tollbooths opened at the end of 1995. Traffic could now speed between the mainland and Skye, but at a price. The tolls were set at the same rate as had been charged on the ferries, which had never been cheap. In the first year of operation more than 612,000 vehicles used the bridge. Protesters claimed the bridge was an extension of the national road network, a public road, and passage along it should be free. The investors wanted to recoup their costs and turn a profit. There was a campaign of non-payment. Over a hundred people were convicted for refusal to pay the tolls. Tempers flared.

After being mauled about, dynamited and concreted, Kyleakin Lighthouse Island was abandoned by the bridge builders. The lighthouse keepers' cottage and the bothy deteriorated, the lighthouse remained unlit, obsolete. The Scottish Office found itself the owner of an island it didn't want while the Northern Lighthouse Board retained a lighthouse it didn't need. The island was put up for sale by public auction, valued at around £40,000 – cheap for a Hebridean almost-isle with million-pound views.

A local, perhaps it was Johnny Ach, contacted the actress Virginia McKenna and begged her to use her influence to save the island from becoming the possession of yet another absentee landlord. McKenna and her husband Bill Travers had connections to the area and had starred in the 1969 film version of *Ring of Bright Water*. And they had a charity, the Born Free Foundation, which campaigned on animal welfare issues. The day before the proposed sale at auction, William, the son of McKenna and Travers, and Director of the Born Free Foundation, faxed the Parliamentary Under Secretary of State at the Scottish Office. Could the island be withdrawn from auction and instead be placed in the hands of a trust (the Kyleakin Lighthouse Island Trust) to be initiated by the Born Free Foundation? It could, and was.

Virginia McKenna's fame and the Foundation's influence attracted funding and support for the Trust and the 'Kyleakin Lighthouse Island Project'. The Northern Lighthouse Board agreed to lease the lighthouse to the Trust for a pound a year, and the Scottish Office paid for the renovation and refurbishment of the lighthouse cottage and bothy.

A steering committee was formed. Johnny Ach was asked to be chairman and in October 1998 the keys to the island were handed to Virginia McKenna by a Scottish Office minister, and custody of the island (now a 'community resource') was given to the communities of Kyle and Kyleakin. A building was leased in Kyleakin to house an interpretation centre – the Bright Water Visitors' Centre – and education packs and publicity material were produced. In 1999 the Trust confidently predicted (based on visitor numbers to tourist attractions on Skye and the number of vehicles using the bridge) that 50,000 tourists would pass through the Bright Water Visitors' Centre in Kyleakin annually. The Kyleakin Lighthouse Island Project would soon be self-funding. A project manager, a centre manager and a warden were recruited.

There was a grand opening of the Visitors' Centre and the island in May 2000 and all went well for two years. But instead of the 50,000 expected, approximately 6,000 people passed through the door of the Bright Water Visitors' Centre each year, and only 600 wanted a guided tour of the island. The start-up funding ran out. Gregory and the centre manager left in 2002. Temporary wardens worked for a season or two and then quit. When Virginia McKenna resigned as a trustee in 2003, support and the fundraising nous of the Born Free Foundation went with her. Other trustees resigned. Susan Browning, a recent incomer to the area, took over the running of the Visitors' Centre, and Johnny Ach took people on tours of the island during his lunch breaks.

In the spring of 2004 Johnny Ach resigned as chairman. A new chairman, John Adamson, and trustees including Pete Baggeley began to take a hand in the day-to-day running of the Centre and the island. A part of the lighthouse keepers' cottage was made available to holidaymakers. A trickle of money from the letting of the cottage, shop sales and tours, and donations from visitors to the Centre flowed into the Trust's deep-in-the-red bank account. By the time I walked into the Centre that rainy day in October 2004 the Trust's fortunes were slightly better than they had been for a long time.

In 2004 the Scottish Executive bought the Skye Bridge from the consortium of private investors for £27 million. On Tuesday, 21 December 2004 the tolls were abolished and the twenty-one locals who had jobs running the bridge and the toll booths became unemployed. Almost everyone was happy, except those who had lost their jobs and those who still had a criminal record for non-payment of tolls.

≈

The island, at the height of summer, with everything growing at full pelt, is awash with life, alive with sound. I found myself surrounded by birds: seed-feeder-hogging greenfinches, piping oystercatchers, chevron-winged guillemots, sauntering crows, shags standing with outstretched wings in the sun. I'd catch the multihued flash of a jay winging its way over to Skye, the flitting glide of a hurrying wagtail, a swallow; the screams of swifts careering high above. A wren would shout its head off, then dodge and hide mute among pink and white dog roses as I passed along the cobbled path. A robin often accompanied me, waiting for titbits, as I tended the paths, making my rounds with wheelbarrow, spade and trowel. And in the mornings the herons made their stately, rather sinister way over the island to the lagoon behind the community centre in Kyleakin, where they spent the days fishing and squabbling before flapping their slow, steady way back home to their heronry.

I bought books to identify what I was seeing: green, looping lacewing larvae and the hairy 'woolly bear' caterpillars of the garden tiger-moth, Scotch argus butterflies, Scotch burnet moths with their natty, crimson-and-green satin wings. Common Blue butterflies were . . . common. Psychedelic red admirals fluttered drunkenly over the old lawn. An invasion of bumblebees came to harvest the honeysuckle and heather that flourished along the bothy steps. On hot days, gangs of black robber flies, legs dangling like parachutists, hovered about and got themselves entangled in hair, zoomed into eyes and fell into cups of tea. And the seals, sluglike when hauled out lounging, galumphing and grunting on the skerries, became so sleek-skinned and doglike when they slithered into the sea and circled the island, their bullet heads bobbing on the surface, eyeing me on my perambulations along the network of paths.

≈

Walking late one evening up the cobbled path from the lighthouse I stopped to lean on the wall to look at the bay below. The rumble of tyres over the bridge had died out hours ago and there was a quiet gentleness to the sea. I hadn't been seduced by the otters in Maxwell's books as so many others had been. His otters had seemed smelly, volatile, high-maintenance creatures – characteristics all too human.

It dived, the sleek black tip of its tail the last part of its anatomy to go under. Its head – that black-button nose, those appraising eyes – reappeared, soundlessly. It was calmly watchful, concentrating. It seemed to perceive all things. It dived again, surfaced and dived, moving silently away towards the rocks by the lighthouse gangway. I crept down the path and peered over the wall again. Nothing. I stole onto the gangway, looked down on either side of the railings, but it had gone. Such stealth. The flowing fluid motion of its body through the water. Such charisma. I was an immediate convert.

Two

HIDDEN ROOMS

Every other Wednesday during the summer, the Wednesday Workcrew – Marcus, a volunteer, and often John Adamson, the newly appointed chairman of the Trust – came to help with the maintenance of the island.

I had first met John one afternoon while I was in the lighthouse shed creating order out of chaos. Pulling out a cardboard box stuffed with car accessories from under the workbench I heard a gentle tap on the open doors and spun around to see a tall elderly man dressed in plus-fours, tweed jacket and brogues. On his head was a deerstalker hat and there was an amused expression on his delicately drawn face. John looked like what he was – a Highland gent. He put a fist to his mouth and gently coughed.

'Hellooo!' he said. 'You must be Dan. I've already heard a lot about you.' He had a soft Lowland accent. 'I've been wanting to come across to the island to see you but sadly my time is rarely my own these days.'

We shook hands, John casting his eyes around the chaos. 'You've already made a good start on things, I see.'

'I want to sort it all out. It all feels . . . unloved.'

John tilted his head. 'Well, there's been no one living here for quite some time now. And we do what we can, the Wednesday Workcrew. But during the summer months with everything growing so fast we're often a week behind. We don't intend the island to look like Inverewe Gardens, but the paths do need keeping clear.'

John had come to the island that day, he said, to plant some nasturtiums in the WI Garden. 'The ladies come to their garden whenever they can, but I'm often persuaded by my wife to tend it in their absence.'

We walked together to the WI Garden. Until his retirement, John had been the doctor in Kyle.

'Did you ever treat Gavin Maxwell?' I asked.

John paused before answering. 'I attended him here on the island once, but his usual doctor was the Glenelg man. A young man – Andrew, was it? – came across in a dinghy to collect me. But Gavin wasn't at all a well man by then.'

'Donald Mitchell, I think it would have been,' I said. 'He was the last otter boy.'

'No, I'm sure it was Andrew, but . . . Well, it was a long time ago now. How the memories fade.'

'What did you make of him?' I asked. 'Gavin Maxwell?'

'I think he was not a happy man, not in himself. There was something missing there. But I found him to be a very honest man, a very . . . interesting personality. And a brave man to face up to death as he did.'

'Jimmy Watt called him a genius.'

'I don't doubt that he was,' John said. 'But a genius doesn't necessarily make for an easy person to live with or to know.'

We reached the little rockery and John withdrew two potted nasturtiums from a knapsack. 'They'll look very well here, don't you think? A little yellow among the purple and white of the heathers.'

I quickly came to look forward to Workcrew Wednesdays. Marcus had been helping with maintenance since the beginning and was always the first to arrive, marching across the bridge from Kyleakin roundabout where the Broadford bus dropped him. With his shaggy dark hair, black-framed spectacles and wispy beard, Marcus looked like the late novelist Iain Banks might have looked on a particularly bedraggled day. Like John Adamson, Marcus possessed a Lowland accent.

Marcus was always keen to get started. He donned overalls and wellington boots, grabbed a spade and a wheelbarrow, a pair of shears and the flamegun and set off along the paths, working until lunchtime. After exactly an hour's break, he would resume his hacking and digging until 4.40 p.m., whereupon he would put away his tools, change out of his overalls and, waving a cheery goodbye, march over the bridge to catch the 5.10 p.m. bus back to

Broadford, where he lived. It was rare for him to initiate conversation. He lived alone and he read a great deal – mainly history books, he told me once. Marcus had a mind for facts and he never missed his appointments with the island.

The first Wednesday that Marcus and John came to the island, the island's paths were overgrown and raggedy still. I had made a start, but the network covered much of the island and the bracken, nettles and brambles were crowding out other plants trying to push through to the light. John spent the day swinging a scythe on the west of the island. Marcus attacked a clump of neck-high nettles in front of the house to reveal a flat area ringed with logs – a promontory overlooking the bay. 'We used to call it Lookout Point,' he said.

After Marcus left to catch his bus I showed John what Marcus had revealed. 'He knows this island better than anyone,' John said.

≈

I returned to the harbourmaster's office and Johnny Ach found me some tide tables. I didn't mention my boat idea and neither did he. Back on the island I pinned the tide tables up on the lobby wall. I got hold of a copy of the Beaufort scale and pinned that up too.

An elderly English couple living in Kyleakin called by with some oak saplings for the island. Well-wishers often donated things – the cottage was furnished from cast-offs. I showed the couple around the island and we sought out suitable places to plant the trees. As we stood by the gate saying our goodbyes I mentioned I was looking for a boat.

'It's the one thing lacking,' I said. 'Every island needs one, don't you think?'

The old man turned to his wife. They looked at me.

'We've got one,' he said. 'A sailing dinghy.'

'It's just taking up space in the garden,' she said.

'We've all the bits and pieces to go with it,' he said. 'And there's an outboard engine.'

'If you're selling!' I said.

We smiled and made faces and blew. Some doors you can push on all you like but they'll never open for you; others you only have to lean on and they fall open, no sweat.

I called on the couple the following day. A fibreglass dinghy rested upside down on the patio. Beside it lay coils of rope, a stick-thin mast, a boom, oars, a dagger board and a bright blue sail spotted with mildew.

The man staggered out of a shed with an ancient Seagull outboard engine. 'Lovely old thing,' he said proudly. '1956!' He rested the outboard on the ground. 'It's a two-stroke, easy to maintain. It worked the last time we used it.

We sat at the kitchen table and haggled hardly at all.

Afterwards the woman turned to me and said, 'Guess how old he is.'

'I can't,' I said.

'I'm eighty-six,' the man said.

His wife beamed.

'My wife is much younger. I was lucky to catch her.' They grinned.

The man pointed to a bottle of tablets on the table. 'I swear by those.' He passed me the bottle. 'She gets them off the internet for me. They keep me youthful. I've lived three lives and I'm still going strong.'

The woman put a hand on my arm. 'He was a policeman, then we moved up here and he became a baker.'

'Now I'm a gardener,' the man said.

'I couldn't be a baker,' I said. 'All those early morning starts.'

'The bridge killed the bakery business,' the man said.

'Kyleakin's dying,' the woman said.

And it was true in a way. The bridge had taken all the business away from Kyleakin. Kyle had a bank, a greengrocer and a butcher, a hardware shop, a garage, two supermarkets and more. Tourists heading to Skye stopped and shopped in Kyle, then drove over the bridge and away. Kyleakin had become a cul-de-sac.

'But I still bake once a week,' the man said, 'for friends.'

'And we've got our dogs.'

'And there's always something to be getting on with in the garden.'

'We're all getting older.'

'Don't you miss England?' I said.

'We don't miss England at all,' the man said.

'All that traffic!' The woman shuddered. 'No one has time for anyone there, and the huge long NHS waiting lists and the knife crime . . .'

'It's a different country to the one we left,' the man said. 'I don't like going back.'

'And our children and grandchildren come up to visit us at least once a year.'

The old man was away somewhere else.

'No,' he said, looking up, 'I don't expect I'll ever go back.'

Marcus and John came to help me get the dinghy back to the island. We puttered across the bridge in my car and loaded up the boat bits. We heaved the dinghy down to Kyleakin Beach. John volunteered to drive the car back to the island. Marcus was keen to come in the boat with me.

We put the floorboards into the boat and slid it into the sea. It floated. I held it steady. As Marcus stepped in he caught one of his oversized wellies on the gunwale and crashed to the bottom of the boat.

'I'm . . . I'm okay!' he called, picking himself up.

'Any water coming in anywhere?'

We examined the inside of the boat, lifted the floor-boards to peer into the shallow bilge.

'No . . . Don't think so.' Marcus looked at me. His natural anxiety was fading into boyish adventurousness. I was pleased.

I passed him the oars, pushed the dinghy further into the sea and leapt aboard. I surveyed the small expanse of water that lay between us and the island.

'Hold on tight, Marcus,' I said and rocked the boat from side to side.

What . . . What're you doing?' Adventurousness vanished. Alarm appeared. I sat down on a thwart.

'Seeing if she leaks. Any water anywhere?'

We sat in silence for a while. I savoured the promise of adventure and freedom. It was my first command. I could circumnavigate the island. I could start exploring the surrounding islands and skerries. I would learn to sail.

The sea sparkled. There was barely a ripple. The mid-morning sun was blasting through a clean dark-blue sky, heating up the cloth of our overalls. It was one of those boundlessly beautiful West Highland days, and I in my boat.

The bleeping safety signal of a reversing lorry sounded out somewhere behind us. The dinghy seemed comfortably afloat. I fitted the oars. I decided not to ask Marcus if he could swim.

I was aware that our progress was likely being followed by a few of the villagers. Both the island and the village were like stages where all our comings and goings were carried out in full view, our lives pieces of theatre, as all lives are. The inhabitants of the island observed and were in turn observed by the villagers. For the benefit of my audience I put some thought into my rowing technique, determined not to catch too many crabs. Marcus sat in the stern quietly marvelling, gripping the transom with one hand, indicating which way to steer with the other.

Halfway across I said, but shouldn't have, 'Don't look down now, Marcus, but just here there's a twenty-metre drop to the bottom of the sea.'

'Right-O!' He smiled grimly and tightened his grip, fixing his gaze on the island ahead.

'Do you not think we should be wearing lifejackets? For health and safety?'

'Nearly there!' I called and rowed a little faster for him, as my car, driven by John, the end of a mast sticking out of a window, passed over the bridge high above us.

≈

One wet afternoon when no one wanted a tour of the island, I climbed the steps to the bothy with the intention of giving it a good clear-out. The building had once been the lighthouse keepers' wash-house and its windows looked straight down Loch Alsh, but today the view was obliterated by rain streaming down windowpanes. The pine-panelled walls were covered in posters identifying wild flowers and fungi, trees, birds and 'Animals of the Hebrides'. Three large desks had been rammed in there – two under the windows on either side of the door and another against the back wall. A map of the island was pinned to the wall and a pinboard was covered with thank-you cards and yellow Post-it notes scrawled with action plans and jobs to be done and photographs of previous wardens with visitors. Dust and cobwebs and dead flies covered the desks and windowsills.

I worked my way through the bothy – dusting, tidying, reading. The wind droned in the chimneys. What to do with a rusting bike with a buckled back wheel, a moth-eaten stuffed polecat, an ancient road atlas, jars of used turpentine, a car hubcab, an oil drum? Do I keep the worn-out gloves and the balding paintbrushes hanging from a string above the storage heater, the torn heavy-duty work jackets sagging off pegs? Where else can I put the paint pots, the cardboard boxes of household cleaning gear, the empty jam jars and tins of industrial grease, the assortment of tools, flowerpots, seashells, dried flowers?

I pulled out a drawer filled to the brim with plastic-bagged owl pellets, pine marten scat, otter spraint and the bones of small mammals.

In the hanging files in the old grey cabinet I found copies of long-dead correspondence. I sat at one of the desks and read, the flagstone floor drawing the cold to my feet through the soles of Gregory's old sea boots.

There were letters from Gregory to nature conservation agencies requesting advice on the most ecologically sound way to 'manage' the flora on the island, and copies of the often terse replies his letters had engendered. 'Don't touch ANYTHING,' the agencies ordered. Gregory wheedled, 'What about the little area over by the . . . ? It can't hurt. It'll improve access . . . allow other plants to flourish.' 'Let the island go back to nature,' was the obdurate order from on high.

But the island wasn't a nature reserve. Susan Browning liked to call it a 'nature haven', which seemed a particularly vague and woolly term to me. People stayed in the house on the island, traffic thundered over it, summer visitors were escorted along the paths that criss-crossed it. And Marcus and I picked up all kinds of garbage from the shoreline that faced the two villages. (The wilder west side of the island was considerably cleaner.) The island was by no means a pristine wilderness, but away from the paths the flora and fauna were carrying on as usual – the brambles, heather and bracken smothering, birds fighting and singing and courting, and the otters slunk around. (By now I had discovered the quiet places they frequented.) We were cohabitants, the flora, the fauna and I.

Other files were filled with paperwork concerning the lighthouse, photocopies of the old Register of Lighthouse

Keepers, or related to funding possibilities – applications to charitable institutions for grants to pay salaries and to help with renovating the lighthouse and its gangway.

There was a file stuffed with rainbow-coloured drawings and paintings done by children at the primary schools in Kyle and Kyleakin to commemorate the grand opening five years before. Drawings of stylized lighthouses and cottages and fishing boats; windswept lighthouse keepers with busty wives, and bridges and otters. The wild imaginings of eight-year-olds who'd now be going through the traumas of puberty.

I found photographs of the cottage taken after the bridge-builders had left – broken doors, boarded-up windows and stripped-bare interiors. There had been grass everywhere then, where now there was a jungle of brambles and bracken. I found a photograph of the rediscovery and uncovering of the cobbled path that ran between the lighthouse and the cottage, another of a bulldozer digging out the steep zigzag path between the slipway and the cottage. There were shots of the bothy before renovation – a slateless roof, blackened fireplaces, a crumbling single-ring cooker under a windowless window; a huge marijuana leaf and the word 'Bud!' daubed in red and green on a wall, a rotting black door with '10' painted on it in white. There were photographs of scaffolding and piles of slates, of builders, of a self-important gull on one of the chimney pots, looking for all the world like a charge-hand, studying the workmen below. There was a batch of photographs of Virginia McKenna arranging articles that she had collected from Maxwell's friends and family for the museum in the Long Room; a photograph of Gregory, in puffer jacket and sea boots, standing by the little motorboat I'd taken to the island in 2001.

In the bottom drawer of the grey filing cabinet I found a telephone answering machine. I plugged it in and pressed a button. 'Hello, this is Gregory Turpin on Kyleakin Lighthouse Island. If you would like to leave your name and number I will get back to you as soon as I can.' I'd met the man, I'd just been reading his letters, scrutinizing his handwriting; seen him in photographs. He'd been the last me. I felt like the Jack Nicholson character in *The Shining* running into ghastly ghostly Delbert Grady in the Overlook Hotel.

JACK: Mr Grady, you WERE the caretaker here.
GRADY: I'm sorry to . . . differ with you, sir, but YOU
    are the caretaker. You've always been the caretaker.

Hearing Gregory's voice on the answering machine, alone in the bothy, gave me the creeps.

Outside, the storm clouds were dispersing as the wind blew them south-east down Loch Alsh. I opened the bothy door and moved my chair to the doorway to breathe in clean air. Hidden in a nearby tangle of brambles the whitethroat was doing its rounds. Its unmistakable lilting song sounded out between drips of stalled rain dropping from the bothy roof. The bothy was full of dead dreams. Where there had once been energy and motivation, there was now only silence and stuff and memories, and me.

≈

The lighthouse on the island was designed by David and Thomas Stevenson, of the famous Stevenson lighthouse-building dynasty (of which the writer of *Treasure Island* and *Dr Jekyll and Mr Hyde*, Robert Louis Stevenson, was also a member). A Stevenson occupied the post of Engineer to the Northern Lighthouse Board – the body responsible for erecting and maintaining lights around Scotland and the Isle of Man – continuously from 1799 to 1938. These days such blatant nepotism wouldn't be allowed, but in fact the Stevensons and the Directors of the Northern Lighthouse Board knew what they were doing. The Stevenson light-houses remain remarkable feats of engineering, and more importantly, have saved lives.

In 1853 a decision was taken by the Northern Light-house Board to light the two narrow channels between Skye and mainland Scotland at Kyleakin, and at Ornsay further down the coast. (Later, in 1910, a tiny lighthouse was erected on one of the islands off Sandaig, and across the water 'Camusfeàrna' house was built for the lightkeeper.) Plans for two identical lighthouse towers and keepers' cottages were drawn up and bricks were shipped to the proposed sites from the nearest brickworks, two hundred miles to the south. By January 1857 the towers had been erected, the cottages built and roofed, and a decision had been made to enclose a third of an acre at each site to create a small walled vegetable garden.

The tower of Kyleakin lighthouse, seventy feet high and built on a platform of natural rock six feet above the high-water mark, shone a fixed beam of white light which in clear weather could be seen for eleven nautical miles. A red sector (panes of red glass filtering the white light) indicated safe passage through the channel. On 10 November 1857 the lights at Kyleakin and at Ornsay were exhibited for the first time. Their lamps were fuelled by sperm oil (from the head of a sperm whale) until 1900, then by paraffin.

For the first 103 years a constantly changing procession of Principal lighthouse keepers and Assistant lighthouse keepers lived in the cottages to look after the light. An Occasional keeper would come over in emergencies or when one or other of the keepers was on leave. Kyleakin Lighthouse Island is a rocky outcrop in the middle of the sea, hammered by salt-laden sea winds and lashed by rain. Any habitation in such an elemental place needs constant monitoring and maintenance. As early as 1866 – only nine years after the light was first lit – an Assistant keeper was complaining to the Commissioners of the Northern Lighthouse Board of 'great damp in my house'.

The light was on permanent standby between dawn and dusk. Before dark the duty lightkeeper switched the lamp over from a pilot flame to let it flash its unique 'character'.*
The light and fuel levels were checked hourly; a spare flashing unit was tested weekly. The Northern Lighthouse Board's supply vessel sailed up from Oban every three months, anchored off the island at high tide and winched supplies ashore (massive mooring hooks, cemented onto the rocks, are still to be seen today, rusting away). The Board's inspectors thought up jobs to keep off-duty keepers busy (an idle mind being the devil's playground): keeping a log of air temperature and pressure, painting and carrying out maintenance of the buildings, spreading lime on the jetty to keep away seaweed, cutting back vegetation, building a wall here and laying a path there, looking after the vegetable garden. And there was always a lot of polishing to be done – of the lens and the windowpanes of the lamp room, of copper piping and the brass handrails and floor surrounds in the tower. The cobbled path between the house and the tower was laid by the lighthouse keepers with pebbles brought across from Kyleakin Beach.

For a Hebridean rock station, with the two villages less

---

* Each lighthouse, lit buoy, light beacon, light vessel, etc., exhibits a unique sequence of light and dark, or flashes (a 'character'), so that at night the mariner can match each particular light (s)he sees with that marked on the sea chart of the vessel, to navigate a safe passage. Lights at night, to a mariner, spell danger.

than a mile away, Kyleakin must have been a cushy posting. And the keepers of Kyleakin Lighthouse were allowed to live on the island with their families, which wasn't the norm. There was a well on the western side of the island, buried beneath the bridge now, along with the walled garden. The keepers grew vegetables, kept hens, went fishing. Hot water was a luxury in the early days, but later a small generator was installed to provide electricity. The families were reliant on a boat to get across to the villages for their canned food and tinned milk, fuel for cooking and heating, and for their mail. At one time there were nine lighthouse keepers' children attending the school in Kyleakin. The school run, especially in the winter, must have been challenging.

In 1960 the Northern Lighthouse Board embarked on a process of automation of their northern lights, and acetylene gas tanks were installed at Kyleakin and Ornsay. The lighthouses became fully automatic, and were reclassified as 'minor lights'. The keepers were withdrawn. Only an Occasional keeper was needed now – to change over the gas tanks when required.

Kyleakin and Ornsay lighthouse cottages were put up for sale by the Board, but they remained vacant and unsold over the next few years, quickly deteriorating, until Gavin Maxwell bought the pair for a knockdown price of £2,000 in September 1963. He only ever owned the cottages and a small piece of ground surrounding them, never the islands. Maxwell employed his acquaintances, Richard Frere and his wife, to redesign the interiors of the cottages and to carry out the conversion work. In 1967 the Ornsay cottage was sold off to help defray some of Maxwell's mountainous debts, but the Kyleakin lighthouse cottage was retained. After he'd acquired the lighthouse cottages, Maxwell (only ever the tenant of the house at Sandaig, never the owner) mentioned more than once his intention to move to one of them in the future, and he favoured Kyleakin over Ornsay.

After Maxwell died in 1969, the Kyleakin lighthouse cottage was bought by Ian Alexander, a sometime acquaintance of Maxwell who was at that time on the staff of Dingwall Academy near Inverness. Alexander brought a donkey over to the island – quite a feat in a small boat – and over the summers of 1970 and 1971 opened the island to the public before selling the cottage on to the actor Michael Bryant, who lived in England and used the island infrequently as a holiday home. In 1981 Alexander and a colleague, Warwick McKean, bought the cottage back from Bryant and negotiated the purchase of the rest of the island, excluding the lighthouse, from the Northern Lighthouse Board. In 1984 they sold the island to Tom Farmer, the Kwik-Fit millionaire, for £58,000. In 1992 the Scottish Executive bought the island from Farmer by compulsory purchase for £127,000, and ran the Skye Bridge through the middle of it. On 31 October 1993 the last Occasional

Keeper extinguished Kyleakin Light. It had been burning, continuously, for 136 years.

There are no manned lighthouses in Britain today. They're all automatic. The last lighthouse keeper of the British Isles was withdrawn from Fair Isle Light in 1998. Seafarers of a certain age still grumble about this. It was reassuring to know, they say, that someone – other than their God – was out there watching over them.

≈

Gavin Maxwell spent the last months of his life on Kyleakin Lighthouse Island and part of the myth will remain there, but it is more strongly linked with Sandaig – the place he called Camusfeàrna in his books. It is a place of pilgrimage for many. I first visited in 1985, the year I left school.

I got a job picking fruit and saved money for camping equipment. I decided I'd get the 'Nightrider' train up to Glasgow and then hitch. Daunting, but an adventure. Then I got cold feet. Hitching alone all that way? My head filled with homicidal maniacs and predatory men in macs. I phoned a friend.

'It's a bit last-minute, isn't it?' But Dara wanted to get away as much as I did.

We sat on our rucksacks in Euston Station and watched desperate men rummaging amongst tired commuters for cigarettes and begging money for drink. On the train north we were kept awake by overexcited returning Scots. We arrived in Glasgow disorientated and shattered. We took another train north into the Highlands proper.

I had never been abroad and the only mountainous region I'd visited was the Lake District. The Highlands were different. The mountains were more dramatic, more barren and more isolated than the sensuous green hills I'd climbed in Cumbria. Scottish mountains were hard as nails. We alighted at Tyndrum and trekked up to the road. We stuck out our thumbs. No one stopped. We started walking. The bleak road wound north around a long, high hill. Our rucksacks slowed our pace. We trudged on into late afternoon. Soon there was nothing but open moorland all around. We pitched the tent, scavenged wood and lit a fire for tea, and crawled into our sleeping bags in the mid-summer, northern twilight.

Rain came during the night and stayed. We ran-walked back to Tyndrum station and caught a train to Mallaig where we crossed the Sound of Sleat to Skye. Pretty white houses and sheep dotted the hillsides. A chair-filling American in a fast Italian car picked us up and dropped us at the village of Isleornsay. I wanted to visit the lighthouse keepers' cottage Maxwell had owned there, but it was impossible to get to. Across the Sound of Sleat we could see Sandaig – the islands, the tiny lighthouse, a little white 'but 'n' ben' cottage – the 'croft' I'd read about in the books. We were close – only a mile away, but by sea, not land.

'Perhaps we could get a fisherman to take us across.'

'You ask.'

'No, you.'

We didn't. We pitched the sodden tent in a field behind a pub in the village and the next day walked on into rain. Our map showed a footpath to Kylerhea. We left the road and got lost amidst meandering sheep tracks. We found a track through conifer forest and followed it. A heavy downpour let up a little. We trudged on through a billowing, diaphanous curtain of drizzle. Clouds of midges waltzed around our heads, bit our faces, crawled down our collars, up our nostrils, into our ears.

'Why? Why did I agree to come here?' Dara spat.

The track led us back to the road. A sign pointed the way to the Kinloch Lodge Hotel. We plodded up and asked a man in the lobby for hot food and something to drink. The man cast an appalled gaze at our dripping hair, over our sodden clothing and our boots and the muddy trail we'd left on his oatmeal carpet. We walked out into the hissing rain. Dara lifted a trouser leg and tugged a leech from his calf.

'We have to go on,' I said. 'There's no going back.'

By Kylerhea we pitched the tent and crawled in. Midges crawled in after us, danced, and fed. When the rain stopped I got up to watch fishing boats and coasters chug through the Narrows between the warmly lit dwellings in Glenelg and Kylerhea. The low-pressure weather system had passed, leaving peace behind it.

We awoke to a clear blue sky but found Kylerhea devoid of a shop. My stomach rumbled. Dara told me to shut up. We squelched down the road to the Kylerhea Narrows and boarded the Glenachulish ferry, and on the other side of the Sound marched in silence the mile to Glenelg. We bought chocolate and sweets and fizzy drinks at the little shop and sat outside in the sun to scoff our treats. Only then did we start speaking to one another again.

We went back in to buy more supplies then pressed on uphill to Tormor, climbed over a forestry gate and followed a track that circled and cul-de-sac-ed through conifer forest until we came to the rough footpath that followed the burn down to the sea.

As we made our way through the trees past telegraph poles and cabling we could hear water crashing in the ravine, and through a gap in the trees I glimpsed Sandaig and my heart beat harder against my chest. Black cattle were grazing down there, some of them standing up to their knees in the sea, waiting to cross to the chain of out-lying islands.

Sandaig looked just as it had in the photos I'd studied so often – a meadow ringed by the sea and a burn. Only the house, which had stood so prominent on the meadow, had gone.

I followed Dara down the mountainside to a fence and a makeshift stile. Two wrist-thick ropes, one above the other, stretched between alder trees on either side of the burn. We wobbled across, gripping the upper rope and sliding our boots along the lower one.

By the remnants of a dry-stone wall there was a cairn topped with an engraved bronze plaque three feet square: 'Edal, the otter of *Ring of Bright Water*, 1958–1968. Whatever joy she gave to you, give back to Nature.' People had placed shells and stones and dried flowers around the edges of the plaque. Offerings. Beside the cairn, a rowan tree was dying while a nearby larch grew tall.

A well-beaten path led through long grass to a telegraph pole and a shoulder-high boulder. There was a small brass plaque cemented to the rock: 'Beneath this stone, the site of Camusfeàrna, are buried the ashes of Gavin Maxwell.'

Offerings had been placed around this plaque too.

Between the boulder and the sea were dunes covered with marram grass and, beyond, a long stretch of sandy beach. In the lee of the conifer-covered hillside that we'd descended, and almost set into it, was the 'croft'. It had recently been painted, and there were electricity and telephone wires leading to it. The windows and the low doorway had metal shutters locked in place over them, making the croft impregnable. Black plastic piping ran from the direction of the burn to feed water to a tap wired to a post. Wooden fish boxes had been stacked nearby and covered with a pegged-down tarpaulin. A gargantuan wooden beam lying on cropped grass under one of the windows formed a natural bench, and I caught a glimpse of my projected future self sitting on it, living in the croft, alone or in company, no matter, and writing – just like Gavin Maxwell did.

We walked along the fence under the hillside. There was a barn, its stone walls crumbling, its corrugated-iron roof close to collapse. We came to a gap in the fence and from the roar I knew we'd found the waterfall.

Maxwell had written a lot about that waterfall, and it was by the waterfall that much of *Ring of Bright Water* was written. Maxwell wrote that he considered the waterfall to be the soul of Camusfeàrna and 'if there is anywhere in the world to which some part of me may return when I am dead it will be there.'

Dara and I slipped on mossy rocks on the path to the waterfall. Water crashed, drowning out all other sounds. Tree trunks, washed downstream by past torrents, lay stranded across its lip, damming the burn below. The barren, leafless conifers blotted out the sun. The waterfall roared in its gloom. I felt watched. A trespasser. If a place can have a soul then Sandaig, I think, has a troubled one.

We pitched our tent out of the way of the midges and cattle, on an outcrop of rock that had a shallow basin of turf at the top of it. We gathered driftwood – mostly wooden fish boxes (there were many back then) – and lit a fire to dry our things. The tide ebbed and uncovered a causeway of fine white sand. The black cattle, their heavy nasal sighing carrying across the water, lumbered through the shallows to browse the grassy islands beyond. Oyster-catchers and ringed plovers and turnstones sped away from them, piping and peeping along the sands.

We stayed a week down at Sandaig. We paddled in the bays and caught crabs to grill on a grate over the fire. We waded through fat fronds of kelp in a transparent sea to the furthest island, where there was a Lilliputian, and locked, lighthouse. We watched yachts anchor for the night in the bay before sailing away in the morning to leave us alone again. A young Frenchman came to camp for a couple of days. He'd read *Ring of Bright Water* and had worked out from the book how to find Camusfeàrna (and packed up and left sooner than he'd intended because of the midges). We frightened ourselves by sticking our heads under the icy flow of the waterfall, the cascading water blinding and deafening us to the dread presence we both felt watched us there. We bathed in its deep dark pool. We sat to admire the gulls twist and cry and cavort; we watched seals bob and loaf and raise their dog-eyed heads to the heavens, and mistook them for otters because that was what we wanted them to be.

We spent hours lying in our sleeping bags in the tent playing cards, bellowing to make ourselves heard over the din of downpours and squally winds slapping and shaking

the sides of the tent. We waited impatiently for bad
weather to pass so that we could light a fire and cook.

One evening after the birds had gone to bed, apart from
the sea kissing the shoreline, there was silence and stillness
all around. No wind. Complete and utter peace. As dark-
ness fell, sprawled by the fire, I told Dara about the curse.

'. . . and she cursed him on that rowan tree, the one we
saw that's dying down by Edal's cairn.'

'But she was a poet, Kathleen Raine,' Dara said.

'She believed she had occult powers.'

'I don't believe in all that stuff.'

'She was in love with him. She believed they were soul
mates. He took the title of *Ring of Bright Water* from one of
the poems she wrote him while staying down here alone
with Mij.'

'How did she do it?'

'It was a wild night.' I intoned, 'Gavin Maxwell and
she had quarrelled, violently, "and she had put her hands
upon the trunk of the rowan tree and with all the strength
of her spirit she had cursed me, saying, 'Let him suffer here
as I am suffering.' Then she had left, up over the bleak
hillside."'

Dara chucked a fish box on the fire. 'And you reckon it
worked?'

'Listen: Mij was killed near here by a road mender soon
after. Gavin Maxwell had a car smash that left him lame,
his health deteriorated, his marriage failed, he became

practically bankrupt. Then the house burned down and Edal was fried alive in the inferno. Gavin Maxwell lost almost everything in that fire. He moved to Kyleakin Lighthouse Island. Eighteen months later . . . he was dead. Think about it. That rowan over there is like a spent force, its badness all used up. That's why it's dying.'

'I've just realized,' Dara whispered, 'Edal's cairn and Maxwell's rock – they're graves.'

'What about ghosts?' I said. 'Do you believe in them? I think ghosts are people who don't know they're dead.'

Maxwell's rock – the site of the house – was just across the burn from us. Before Gavin Maxwell and the others lived in it, there were lighthouse keepers and their families living there.

'Gavin Maxwell wrote about there being a poltergeist in the house,' I said. 'He experienced ghostly activity in there at first hand. He also wrote about a murder that took place in one of the caves just down the coast. Before the Highland Clearances there were houses all around here. You can still see the bumps in the ground where they were. People would have died down here – of old age, famine, drowned while out fishing. Now there's nothing. Just us.'

'Where did you get all this?'

'The books.'

The fish box caught fire and a tower of flame leapt into the air with a whoosh, lighting the rocks and sea around us.

'I didn't say anything earlier,' Dara said, 'but this morning when I was getting water from the burn I saw a man walking along the beach by the croft. He had a dog with him but it wasn't *like* a normal dog. It was small and black and it had a long flattish tail. And it didn't move like a dog. I only saw them for a second. I bent down to fill up the billycan and when I looked back they were gone.'

'The waterfall scares me,' I said.

'I think they might have been *spectres*.'

'Did you *really* see someone down there this morning?'

'I wouldn't camp down here on my own, would you?'

We lapsed into silence and stared into flames. Beyond the threshold of light around us was utter darkness. Uncertainty, then fear, crept over us like Nosferatu creeping up the stairs. We retreated to the tent on the rock, where we had an all-round view and where no one and nothing could get at us.

We walked back over the hills to Glenelg to buy more supplies and to visit the dingy, smoke-stained pub. We ate lunch and played pool and were served, begrudgingly, beer. Burly, unsmiling men sat at the bar and crowded us out when we ordered. Did they remember Gavin Maxwell? Had they liked him? Was one of those men the one that killed Mij? But I asked them nothing, as we were silently told that the likes of us were not wanted here.

Returning to the sea and seclusion of Sandaig we came

across a couple of pensionable age standing by Maxwell's grave.

'You've made the pilgrimage too, have you?' the woman asked.

'Yes,' I said.

'No,' said Dara.

'It's lovely down here,' said the man.

They knew a lot about Gavin Maxwell. 'And have you read *The White Island* and *Maxwell's Ghost*?' the woman asked.

I hadn't. I knew that *Raven Seek Thy Brother* was the last book Maxwell ever wrote. A fire destroyed the house at Sandaig and then Maxwell moved to Kyleakin Lighthouse Island. He died a year later, aged fifty-five. The end. That was all I knew. Sixteen-year-olds lack a certain nuance in their thinking.

After Sandaig burnt down, the couple told me, Maxwell had hit on the idea of establishing a wildlife park on Kyleakin Lighthouse Island. 'Come and visit the island home of a famous author and view his private collection of Scottish fauna.' The other otter, Teko, had survived the fire and was to be, along with Maxwell himself, the star attraction. Maxwell employed a young naturalist, John Lister-Kaye, to supervise the project, but died before the wildlife park was finished. After Maxwell's death, Lister-Kaye had stayed on in the Highlands to write *The White Island*, about his time living at Kyleakin.

Maxwell's Ghost was by Richard Frere, who converted the lighthouse cottages and later became Maxwell's business manager and trusted confidant, one of the few who could reason with Maxwell and calm him down.

'That one especially will tell you a lot about Gavin,' the woman said. 'He was a very mixed-up man.'

'They're not too keen on him in the village,' the man said. 'Never were. The man Gavin accused of killing Mij still lives there actually.'

'Big Angus?'

'I'm not sure that's his real name,' the man said. 'The lady in the shop told us he never touched Mij and that Gavin had a grudge against him about something else. She said to us: "That Gavin Maxwell with his books has made that man's life a misery."'

The couple told me that the croft I coveted was owned by a master at Eton, who lived in Wales and used it only occasionally.

'Look at this place, so desolate and abandoned now, and yet his books about Sandaig are full of incident,' the man said.

'You'd never believe it,' the woman said. 'It's a little like after the waiters have cleared away a table in a restaurant. You'd never know that just a few moments ago there'd been a couple sitting there having a blazing row.'

'We're soon cleared away,' the man said.

The woman looked down at the plaque on the boulder. 'Aren't these offerings of flowers and shells and things . . . odd? Gavin touched a nerve, didn't he, and got on more than a few people's nerves. I'm not sure what he would have made of these.'

'A moody man,' I said.

'An unhappy man,' the woman said, 'with secrets.'

I wondered if they had known him, for they had called him Gavin, but before I could ask they had waved and were walking away.

Dara and I were getting on each other's nerves. We ran out of firewood. It was Dara's turn to get more.

'If you want it, you get it,' he said.

'But it's *your* turn.'

Dara said nothing.

I stomped off across the burn. It was running high from an incoming tide and the day's rain. I stumbled on the loose rocks, soaking my socks and trouser legs. Each time we'd collected driftwood we'd had to search further along the shore. By the time I'd lugged as much driftwood as I could carry back to camp I felt done in, beaten – by the weather, the midges, by Dara's moodiness and by the cold and damp and the sheer isolation of Sandaig.

'Perhaps we should leave tomorrow,' I said.

I eyed the croft and wished I was in it.

'Good idea,' said Dara.

Dara talked all the way to Glenelg about the humungous meal he was going to order in the pub.

'Real food and loads of beer. And maybe a whisky chaser. Gavin Maxwell liked his whisky, didn't he? Let's drink a drink to him.'

We were underage, but silly laws like that didn't seem to apply up there.

When we got to the pub, the doors were locked and the lights were off. We walked down the road to the shop but that was closed too.

'Sunday,' I said.

'I know,' Dara said, 'but pubs don't shut on Sundays.'

A man was standing in the road. We went up to him.

'It's a Sunday,' he said.

'We know,' we said.

'Well then!' he said, as if that put an end to the matter.

'Will the pub be open later?' Dara asked. 'This afternoon? Tonight?'

'Are you daft? Am I having to spell it out? You'll NOT be getting served on the Sabbath!'

'We only want to buy food,' I said, but the man was striding away, shaking his head.

Bitten half to death by midges, we hastily erected the tent beneath dripping trees on the outskirts of Glenelg and lay silently fuming in our sleeping bags, counting down the hungry hours until we could away to a place with shops and cafes, where we could find a coach to take us south, where nature had been tamed, the weather was clement, and where Sundays weren't very special any more.

I remember the ride in the post bus the next morning. I remember a big man gripping the steering wheel in one fist while smashing the windscreen with the other, trying to kill a fly that, he informed us, had been trying his patience all morning. I remember my fear mixed with admiration of a man who could drive so carelessly yet so accurately along the single-track roads and spindly bridges over the Ratagan Pass to Kyle of Lochalsh. There was no Skye Bridge back then. Ferries ran the half-mile of sea between Kyle and Kyleakin. I may have asked about getting across to the island, but it was private property. We caught a coach to Glasgow and took a night train south, our carriage filled with Scots, already homesick, drinking and singing their way down to London.

≈

All my life I've read books, like a dervish turns circles, constantly, unremittingly. I lose myself in a book until my eyes bleed (figuratively speaking, of course) and still I read on, projecting myself into adventures, other people's stories. Yet all that first summer on the island I never finished a book. I was too busy, too preoccupied, always learning something new. Someone might arrive on the island at any moment. I had work to do and people to see and by the end of each day I'd be exhausted by the demands of the island and the sea air. It was all I could do to cook a meal before falling into dreamless sleep. For once in my life I knew what it was to have *purpose*. Up until then, my life had been goal-orientated, which is all very well, but once you achieve a goal, or fail, what then? Set yourself up with another? Set yourself up to win, or lose? Over and over? I took tours of the island, chopped and cleared, tidied and cleaned. It was very pleasant to feel like a homeowner, house-proud. Island-proud.

And I couldn't settle to write anything either. I needed long, uninterrupted stretches of time and a kind of boredom that came from loneliness and a lack of interest in the people and places around me. People kept saying, 'Oh, the island must be a wonderful place for writing, all that solitude.' And the island appeared to be the perfect writer's retreat – an inspiring view, the tranquillity, the 'splendid isolation', a place to lock oneself away. But there was always something else I could be doing. The island was a project without end. The book I'd begun in India remained locked up in my laptop. Not forgotten exactly, but dormant.

Beyond our northern land of sea and rock and sudden squalls, the busy world south of us still turned. The earth spun and the summer moved on; the days shortening, the nights growing incrementally colder. The moon waxed and waned and the island expanded and shrank with the tides. Sometimes it seemed so small when the sea crowded its shore; and at others so big when a dead low tide revealed the sandbanks and shoals around it. The island changed continually.

I was always stopping to look in those days, looking through binoculars, as I circled the island time and again. I'd read how lighthouse keepers, having plenty of time on their hands, made a habit of walking ever so slowly around their rocky islets in order to notice everything, the infinitesimal changes that all add up to the totality of a turning cycle of seasons. On wet days I'd sit on a chair in the lobby with the door open, alive to all the movement amidst the stillness around me – the birds and animals and humans, the sea lapping, rising, falling, crashing. And at night I'd walk the island along moonlit paths, as vast container ships, the reflections of their deck lights flickering on wavelets, passed me by on their way to who knew where.

During those first months on the island, I was often reminded of an interactive computer game I used to play at university. The game, *Myst*, unfolds at its own pace. The player is alone on an island of deserted buildings and unpeopled paths. There's a lighthouse, a hut in a forest, a clock tower, a library, a wrecked ship on a beach. Nothing by way of explanation – no backstory, no instruction – is given to the player; there are no obvious goals or objectives, no enemies or threat of death. The player is left to explore the island, the scenery, the buildings and books. The soundtrack to the game is important, for it holds clues.

As you travel around, you hear the sea, gulls, the wind; the squeak of rusty hinges, the turning of the pages of the books in the library, the roar of a furnace in a boiler room. The history of the island is revealed and the puzzle is solved through patience, observation and logic (and, in my case, a website that walked me through when I ran out of ideas). You find clues, discover hidden rooms.

I strolled the island at low tide and high, beneath blue skies by calm seas, in gales and in hissing rain. I stood by the lighthouse when waves bashing into its base ricocheted clouds of spray high into the air, and spindrift blew ashore to spatter the ground all around me. Gulls hovered above me. The soundtrack to my days was of wind on water, wind in my ears, the crash of waves and the cries and babble of birds. There was a notable lack of human chatter. Like *Myst*, the island drew me in and immersed me in its world. Here, too, in the real world, I was look-ing for clues, memories, mementoes. I explored and rooted around. I came to know every inch of that island. But sometimes I wondered what it was I had come there ex-pecting to find.

The island was practically self-sufficient. If I found myself in need of, say, a bracket to fix the split in the door of the hide, or paint or filler, or a plank of wood or tools, screws, nails, bolts, a Petri dish, information to help iden-tify a newly discovered plant or insect, I had only to root around or wait a day or two for inspiration before I'd find what I needed. Or something I could refashion to fit my purpose. I was always coming across things and thinking, *Could be useful. I'll put it up in the bothy.*

I found echoes of the past everywhere. As I cleaned and cleared out and rearranged I came across objects previous occupants had left behind: in a tiny cupboard in the lobby a pair of heavy leather 1930s walking boots; on a ledge above a door my prying fingers found a key that fitted no lock; under a sink a square of black card with a tiny whisky bottle glued to it and the words 'Break Glass in an Emergency'; a Welsh love spoon and another that had been whittled from the board of a fish box. A scrunched-up piece of paper sticking out from under the washing machine in the kitchen read: *Gregory, Can you pick us up a couple of bottles of wine (white) when you're next in Kyle. Thanks xx.* Another piece of paper, fished out from under a desk in the bothy, had a drawing of a yacht and a smiley face: *Gone sailing. See you later xx.*

In the evenings I sat on Maxwell's old sofa in the silence and antique smell of the Long Room and read comments left by the work parties in the first visitors' books: of midge-bitten days spent laying the paths and pulling bracken and erecting safety barriers along cliff edges, of drunken marches back from the pubs, of evenings by fires and singsongs and leaving parties.

≈

One day in August I was up in the bothy helping Susan Browning dump some clutter she'd brought across from the visitors' centre.

'Even if you're not here this winter the bothy gets damp and will need airing and drying out.'

I mumbled something about staying on the island a little while longer if possible.

'I can't imagine you'd cope all alone on the island. Not after all those exotic places you've been to. The winters up here just go on and on. It can rain for weeks at a time. And there won't be any tours to take. The Centre will be closed. It can be very isolating, you know.'

'It would be a perfect time to get on with my book,' I said. 'There's so much more needs doing to get the island looking good again.'

'Oh, I can't think about that now,' Susan Browning said, pushing an armful of old blankets at me and bustling off down to the cottage.

An old friend telephoned to see how I was getting on. 'You live *under a bridge*? Just like the troll in "Three Billy Goats Gruff". How long will you stay?'

'Forever.'

Three

STAYING ON

Sandy Wood looked like a seafaring Santa Claus who'd delivered the Christmas presents far too early and now had almost a year to potter about looking for something useful to do. He was all pale pink skin and Captain Birdseye beard, and he had one of those bizarre hairstyles that some middle-aged men go in for – bald on top, with the silver-grey hair on the side of his head grown long and pulled back into a ponytail, which he kept in place with a purple rubber band. But most of all, and most importantly, Sandy Wood had *time*.

I'd spied him on several occasions over the summer, criss-crossing the loch between Kyleakin and Kyle, darting around the deck of a classic wooden yacht in a padded plaid shirt and yellow fisherman's boots. Once or twice he had come into the visitors' centre while I was there gossiping with Susan Browning. He'd stroll in out of the rain to use the lavatory, dressed in oily jeans and with a shiny black sou'wester on his head, bringing with him easy pleasantries and a strong smell of bilge – that not-altogether-unpleasant odour of seawater and diesel and dust.

'That's Sandy,' Susan Browning had said the first time. 'He lives on *that*,' and she had pointed through a window to a despondent fishing trawler, indelicately draped with blue plastic sheeting, leaning drunkenly against Fisherman's Wharf. 'It's called *Ebb 'n Flow*. He's converting it into a sail-training vessel. Very slowly.'

Rowing my dinghy around the island, using it to collect the flotsam and jetsam that washed ashore, visiting the villages in it rather than walking, I felt I was becoming an islander. But the 1956 Seagull outboard engine the old man had given me refused to run. I'd tried everything. I'd found a website devoted to Seagull engines and fired off questions to the enthusiast who ran it. The man responded promptly and I had learned a lot about Seagulls, but still couldn't get mine to go. A man like Sandy, I reasoned, a man who really *knew* boats, surely he'd know what to do.

One evening, after yet more fruitless tinkering – the Seagull laid out in the bothy on a length of old sheet like a body on a shroud – I drank several large glasses to effect some Dutch courage and set off over the bridge.

Unlike the boats and the tides around her, *Ebb 'n Flow* never moved. Fisherman's Wharf, lit by yellow streetlights, was piled high with plastic fish boxes, rope, oil drums and lobster and crab pots. It was low tide. *Ebb 'n Flow* lay far below the level of the wharf. There was a ladder.

I clambered down the greasy rungs and climbed over the gunwales of the trawler. The deck of *Ebb 'n Flow*, under the plastic sheeting, was covered with a mountain of gear: half a canoe, old doors, wheel-less wheelbarrows, a Porta-loo cabin, pieces of iron and old engines, a ten-foot-high jumble of timber. I picked my way to the wheelhouse where I was met by a large athletic trailhound. It planted its paws on the deck and studied me. I banged on the wheelhouse window. The dog and I exhaled plumes of smoke into the night air.

One of those furry Russian hats moved across the window and I heard the squeak of hinges and footsteps clattering on loose planking. Sandy, looking like an émigré, appeared behind his dog. I launched into the story of the Seagull. Sandy stood by his dog, weighing me up as I bleated out my tale of frustration and woe. It occurred to me that I wasn't going to be invited below decks for a drink. The water in the harbour around us was still and slick, black like treacle. My voice, thickened and made immoderate by drink, echoed over the water into the empty village streets.

'Anyway, I was wondering whether you could take a look at it sometime.' I nodded at the piles of gear. 'You look like a handy bloke. You know about boats. You *must* know about outboards.'

I can't remember Sandy's reply, just his adroit handling of a tipsy man and how he coaxed me off his boat with a response that was both encouraging and deeply non-committal. He told me he would come to the island and I walked home greatly encouraged, but when I got back in my room, I realized he'd never said when.

Some weeks later, the Seagull burst into life. I'm not sure what it was that I did, but whatever it was, it worked. I took long exploratory trips down Loch Alsh and puttered up the coast to Plockton. The Crowlin Isles beckoned, but the six miles of open sea between us always felt a tad too far for my little plastic boat and its antique engine.

One of the trustees owned a smart yellow sailing boat. He invited me to sail with him in a couple of races organized by the Kyle Flotilla – a bunch of local sailors. His yacht was a fast little thing and we did very well. One Saturday morning, when a strong wind was blowing and bad weather forecast, I telephoned to see if a planned race, the last of the season, was still on. It was. But at Kyleakin marina – pontoons and boats alive with competitive men in waterproofs readying their yachts for the race – the trustee stood inscrutable beside his little yellow yacht. We stepped aboard. We hauled the outboard from the bowels of the boat and fixed it in its bracket. The big man fussed with the engine, pressed the starter button. The outboard wouldn't go. I set about hanking a foresail onto its stay. The weather was drear. Rain came to keep the half-gale company.

Sandy skipped past dressed in an all-in-one waterproof overall, a mad glint in his eye. 'Cracking day for a sail,' he called cheerfully. 'Lively!'

The trustee was huffing with the outboard, which still wouldn't start. Sandy's yawl, *Emma Gaze*, was moored ahead of us. A man possessed, Sandy was rushing about on board, chattering excitedly to his crew, hauling on ropes and shouting out bons mots to the other skippers readying their yachts in the wind and rain. The trustee called me back into the cockpit. The outboard was broken and we wouldn't be racing that day. Sandy, overhearing, immediately invited us to sail with him.

Emma Gaze was ramshackle – all frayed ropes and mildewed sails, oily bilge water and rusty tools. The whole enterprise was run on thrift – massive fishing buoys used for fenders, a cranky old VHF radio. Sandy used bits of rope and knots where richer skippers would use 'a piece of kit'. The inside of *Emma Gaze* was a mess. No comfort down there, nowhere to sit, or lie.

'I'm doing her up,' Sandy called when he saw me peering down the companionway. '*Emma Gaze* is living proof you don't need to be a millionaire to go sailing,' Sandy said when the trustee commented on the storm-tossed state of everything. 'I beg and I borrow,' he raised a finger, 'but I've never stolen a thing in my life.'

Sandy's crew that day was a man called Pat, the warden of the youth hostel in Kyleakin. Myopia and spectacles in the rain are a problem, and Pat stumbled about the boat like a blind man. Pat wasn't tall and had been dressed by Sandy in extra-large fluorescent orange oilskins. He was very cold, very wet, and for some reason that day (he didn't usually) resembled one of the seven dwarfs.

Sandy coaxed *Emma Gaze*'s inboard engine into life and we throbbed out of the marina and into the Kyle, ready for the starting gun. The rain fell steadily and my outdoor-adventure shop waterproofs quickly became soaked through and useless. Sandy put Pat on the helm. The trustee grimly hung on to jib sheets. We tacked up and down behind the starting line. I pushed a sail up to Sandy through the forward hatch and noticed how huge his hands were – mangled and gnarled like lumps of beaten steak, or those dried hams you see hanging in hypermarkets in France.

The wind swung around to the west and blew harder.

The starting gun was fired and we raced up Loch Alsh to round marker buoys and islands. *Emma Gaze* was a heavy boat. We fell far behind the others. A staysail blew apart, ripping open from bottom to top like a zip. I clawed forward with Sandy to grapple the wildly flapping sail down on deck. *Emma Gaze* was heeled so far over I could practically walk up the mast. Sandy and I hollered at each other, blasted by the wind and the spray and rain as we fought the tattered sail; we yelled to make ourselves heard over the insane clattering of halyards, the humming sails, the scream of the wind through the rigging, the sea sluicing down *Emma Gaze*'s decks. And I found myself laughing, loving the thrill of it all, alive and heroic.

We didn't finish the race till late afternoon, long after the rest of the flotilla had repaired to sip hot toddies in the bar of the Lochalsh Hotel. When we staggered bedraggled into the bar, just before prize-giving, we were met with an almighty cheer.

We didn't win a prize.

Visitor numbers to the island and the Centre tailed off as soon as the school summer holidays drew to a close. Towards the end of October the tours came to a complete stop. Susan Browning decided to close the visitors' centre. It wouldn't reopen till Easter.

For a week or two I felt restless and unwanted. There was little for me to do. The telephone didn't ring. The cottage remained unlet. I remained unsummoned and my future remained uncertain. Susan Browning and the trustees hadn't decided, it seemed, whether I should stay or go. I wandered the island, explored the coastline in my dinghy and cogitated. Without others to bounce ideas off, left alone without occupation or purpose, negatives came cantering into my mind like runaway horses, tethers and chains trailing after.

The hills seemed to wither and shrink a little. Days became shorter, nights colder. Mist crept over the hills and lingered low on the mountainsides, blotting out the high tops and wafting across the island like smoke. On such days an oppressive silence and loneliness clung to the villages and I'd fret about seeing the sun ever again. A sleek, matt-black torpedo – a lone submarine – crept around on manoeuvres under grey mists out in the Inner Sound. Then a westerly breeze would pick up and begin raging, ripping leaves from trees and flattening what was left of summer blooms, churning the already racing sea to an angry grey. Bunches of rowanberries littered the island's paths.

One moonless night, a banshee screeching outside the house awoke me. A south-westerly was blowing hard. I got out of bed and opened the door of my room and stood naked before the gale. The bleached stalks of long-dead fireweed by Lookout Point bowed to the ground. I pulled on trousers and sea boots and pushed around the back of the house, shivering as I stood listening to the sibilant shrieking through the wire-mesh barriers on the bridge above me. It was the cry of the violently insane, this end-less beseeching screaming. South-westerlies were always angry.

An area of sea called the Minch, to the north-west of the island, acts like a funnel, channelling wind and waves down the Inner Sound into Loch Alsh. After a gale, rollers – great undulating lumps of oily green sea – rush under the bridge to crash onto the beach at Kyleakin, grab fist-sized pebbles and drag them down into the deep. These rollers, these echoes of ferocious storms in the North Atlantic beyond the Minch, can continue for days. Then the sea round about settles down and there's a respite of a few days, when the atmosphere is so washed clean that there's a crisp clear view for miles. Then another low-pressure system comes in off the Atlantic and the cycle of mizzle and gales starts over again.

The grass had stopped growing. Species of bird that had been common around the island became scarce; others took their place. Robins and greenfinches went. Chaffinches and dunnocks came by. A coal tit skittered in the rosebush vacated by the wren. Guillemots, having spent the summer skimming low over the sea in fast-flying flocks, disappeared. The shags left their summer haunt in the Inner Sound to paddle inshore and explore the more sheltered bays around. The dockens were dying; rosebay willowherb had already shed its cotton wool and withered. The brambles, useful for once, sprouted berries. The briars stopped creeping, the foxglove petals fell, rosehips reddened. The montbretias still flashed their fire, but all over, the colours of summer were faltering, fading, like lights going out one by one.

I set to work reinstating the lighthouse keepers' lawn in front of the house, working my way down the bank to where the heather and blueberries began. I chopped and raked and wheelbarrowed away. From the hills above

Kyleakin I began to hear low, gargling roars, like an elongated cough of a bull. I scanned the hills with binoculars but saw only the muted palette of autumn.

One Saturday, feeling terribly alone, I trekked into the Kintail hills. Up there on the high tops, two hours' walk in from the nearest road, you become a nothing in a landscape more uncaring than your worst enemy. The weather, the terrain – none of it gives a damn about you or the rest of humanity, though it's nothing personal. One day the world will shake itself and we humans will come to grief just as the dinosaurs did. But the hills and the wind and the waters will remain, long after we're gone.

As I tramped up a hill I looked to its summit to see thirty hinds – female red deer – ears pricked with curiosity, staring straight down at me from the skyline. Then I spotted the stag, strutting back and forth beside his ladies, glaring at me, daring me to come closer.

On the way down from the tops I fell back into the drenched hillside to watch two stags on either side of a gorge goading each other. They bellowed, trotted along the hill, roared and trotted back the other way, mirroring. The ravine was wide and deep; there was no way they could get to each other. But they roared anyway, crazed with testosterone, ready to fight, vital.

I went to work on my book and spent several hours of each day up in the bothy, preparing my opus for publication, tidying up paragraphs, sweeping sentences. I was impatient now to get on with my writerly career. I was still, in those days, pursuing the notion of writer as romantic icon. I had simply to write a bestseller, gain a vast global audience (by breaking America of course – just like the Beatles, Oasis, Led Zeppelin . . .) and accrue great wealth and acclaim. Gavin Maxwell had done it; I could do it. (Of course I'd be far shrewder than he, financially. He was always broke.) The life of a writer had always seemed to me to be ideal. You worked alone, had no boss, no set hours. You were free to travel. Pen could be put to paper anywhere in the world. And when at last one tired of fame, and the bohemian whirl of louche literary parties became tiresome one could, like my fellow scribes J. D. Salinger, Thomas Pynchon and B. Traven, retreat from one's public and become 'an enigma'.

An organization supporting the arts in the Highlands offered writers a critical-appraisal service for works-in-progress. I sent Hi-Arts the opening chapters of my book. I researched literary agencies, composed covering letters and a synopsis and printed off copies of the first three chapters of my magnum opus, my vade vecum of the road. I stuffed my not-so-little bundles of hope into padded envelopes, rowed across to the post office in Kyle to buy stamps (return postage included), and slotted my dreams into the chipped salty maw of the rusty red pillar box. The decision to row across to Kyle, rather than take my car or walk, was an important part of the process. It fitted with the romance of the thing. It might even persuade those in charge of my destiny, whoever they may be, to pull a few strings.

I was ready. I'd been ready for the onslaught of fame and fortune for years.

≈

One of the trustees knew a stalker who worked a large estate some miles from Kyle of Lochalsh. I mentioned I was keen to go stalking. I was interested in spending a day working the hills, instead of tramping over them as a rambler. The trustee put me in touch and early one grey late-October morning I met Ewan at the gate. He was a few years older than I. Solidly built.

'Ewan's family are hill folk,' the trustee had told me. 'They go back generations here.'

We made small talk in the Land Rover as we struck out north-west.

'Gavin Maxwell gave my dad a lift home from the station once,' Ewan said. 'He came in for a whisky or two, sat chatting. My dad thought him all right; a good talker.'

We turned off the main road and powered over Beinn Raimh. The clouds were being blown apart and a cold sun was peering through. We took a side road and drove along a single-track road. We came to a lodge with fairytale turrets and Ewan steered the Land Rover into a courtyard.

A rangy man with smooth white hair and military bearing stepped from an outbuilding.

'He used to be something in London,' Ewan murmured.

The owner hailed Ewan, shook my hand. He seemed unsure of me, or farouche.

'He lives on Kyleakin Lighthouse Island,' Ewan explained. 'Where Gavin Maxwell used to live.'

'Oh yes?' the owner said, vaguely interested. 'We went to see Maxwell at his house down at Sandaig once. A strange fellow, I thought. He had some very strange friends too.'

The owner left us. Ewan unloaded gear from the Land Rover.

'I've got this for you,' he said, handing me a deerstalker. 'It breaks up your profile on the hill.'

I'd brought a stick, walking boots and gaiters, an old waxed jacket, binoculars, and lunch.

'Otherwise you're dressed fine. It's a long walk up.'

He shouldered a rifle case and a knapsack and we started up the side of the hill. The mountains above us cast a shadow over the fairytale turrets below. We slowly traversed the hillside.

'I've travelled a fair bit myself,' Ewan said. 'China, America. I take my lads with me. Aye, we've seen some of the world.'

I thought at first this was mentioned defensively but, in contrast to many of the white settlers I had met, Ewan was comfortable in himself. He was happy to tell about his life and family and the more we blethered as we climbed, stopping now and then to rest, the more Ewan told.

'When I was seventeen I got a job on a boat out of Kyle. Johnny Ach, you know, the harbourmaster in Kyle, got me the job. It wasn't much of a job but it was money and we sailed down to England. I signed off the boat and worked a year or so down there, the usual – labouring, factory work, manual, unskilled. Then one day my dad phoned. He'd always worked on the railway, driving the trains between Kyle and Inverness. There was a job going as a train driver alongside him. He told me to come home. So I came back. I got married and we had kids straightaway. They've left school now, one's a ghillie and the other's an apprentice butcher.'

Driving trains seemed to me a dull job, trundling along the same length of track all week; like lorry driving, only worse because you were always passing the exact same places. Ewan's obvious contentment with such a dull occupation depressed me a little.

'Naw, it's a good job! And the salary's very good for up here.'

He told me how much he was earning.

'Aye, I get by,' he smiled. 'And the trip changes with the seasons. There's always something to see. The colours change, there're eagles and deer along the way, walkers on the hills, rainbows, snow, all kinds of weather. I'm busy and well paid. I take my leave over the stalking season. I wouldn't want it any other way. I'm lucky, and more than that, I've got the sense to know it.'

Ewan took paying guests out to 'bag a stag'.

'Some are arrogant, but most are fine. There's good and bad everywhere. On the hill most of us are looking for the same thing.'

The guests paid well and were an important source of income. A Highland estate seems a grandiose, extravagant plaything: the preserve of the very rich; and of course it is. A rich man's folly, for most estates run at a loss. And the Highland Clearances – which by the mass eviction of Highland families created these estates – were a crime. The remains of those settlements can still be seen in forgotten glens: stone walls and the outline of blackhouses – bumps on the ground under turf. North America was peopled by the refugees from these pogroms, many left by ship from the pier at Isleornsay. The hands on the world's clock turn. Those settlements won't be rebuilt, the emigrants won't be returning. The past, like the Caledonian Forest, is gone forever. There is no going back. Today, whatever else we may think about the people who own them, Highland estates provide employment for local people and bring money into the local community.

Ewan knew everyone in the villages around Kyle. I told him what one of the locals had said one evening in the Lochalsh Hotel.

'Where do you belong?' she'd asked, and I couldn't tell her. 'Where are you from?' or 'Where do you live?' was easy, but as to where I belonged . . . So I'd asked the woman where *she* belonged.

'Well,' she said, 'I *belong* down at Killilan in Kintail. It's a small place. There were a few houses there when I was small – all gone – and an Arab owns the Killilan estate now, but I *live* in Kyleakin, since a long time.'

I understood the difference, but I still hadn't an answer for her.

Ewan and I rested for a moment, looking out from the shadow of the mountain down to the frost-sparkled pasture and sunlit lochans far below. A car sped along a black road that ran parallel to the mountainside, the timbre of its tyres deepening for a second as it zipped across a cattle grid. Three or four smallholdings ran in a neighbourly line along the roadside.

'My family are from there,' Ewan said, pointing at the crofts with his stick. 'My dad was the stalker here before me, and my granddad before him. It was a different country up here, even just a few years ago. A lot's changed. Donald John used to be the shepherd here. He lived in that byre we passed.' A derelict barn, its frameless window sockets open to the wind and rain, its floor knee-deep in compacted sheep droppings.

'He slept on a platform above the sheep and at night the heat coming off them kept him warm. He had nothing

really. No one did, except the landowners. When my parents were getting married my dad came up the hill to ask
Donald John to their wedding. Donald said he wouldn't go
but wouldn't give a reason. So my mum went to him and
eventually he said it was because he didn't have the suit to
go in. My dad went back to him. "If I get you the suit,
will you come?" Donald said he wasn't sure, what with the
sheep to look after and so many things to get done while
the weather held. But my parents got him the suit anyway
and took it to him and Donald went to the wedding. After
the dancing he kissed my mother and said he'd not have
missed it for the world. We buried him in that suit.'

'Talking of sheep,' I said, 'I was walking along the
Plockton road once in a bit of a bad mood and passed a
load of sheep. "Look at you," I said to the nearest one, "by
God you're stupid," and as one they all stopped chewing
and glared at me. Spooked me, it did. I apologized immediately and they all turned away and got chewing again.'

'Aye,' Donald chuckled, 'they're not as glaikit as some
suppose.'

We passed an Argo – an all-terrain amphibious vehicle
with outsize knobbly tyres. We were approaching the
summit now and we walked in silence.

Ewan slowed his pace, extended an arm and motioned
that we stop. We dropped into the heather.

Following Ewan's lead, I put my binoculars to my
eyes. We were high now and looked over the tops of the

mountains on the other side of the glen to the mountains beyond. The sun had breached the crest of the hill we'd been climbing and shone on moorland some distance away. Three hinds lazed in the sun, chewing the cud, their backs to us, looking towards the other side of the glen. I ranged my binoculars right. A stag was swaggering crazily, strutting about near the hinds.

'See him?' whispered Ewan. 'A seven- . . . *eight*-pointer.'

Between us and the deer lay muddy peat hag and bog.

Ewan slid his rifle from its case, checked it and slid it back.

'Keep behind me. The wind is coming from them to us. They can't smell us.'

We scrambled around the peat hags, bent low, moving slow, keeping an eye on the deer. The hinds remained oblivious. The stag trotted towards the hinds. The hinds stood.

'He's getting ready to have a go at one of the hinds. We've to be quick.'

We moved forward and came to a neck-high bank. Ewan crouched and withdrew the rifle from its case. I squatted. Ewan rose and fired two rounds.

'I'm sorry,' Ewan said, turning to me, 'I wasn't thinking. Did you want . . . ?'

I stood and saw the fallen stag, the hinds cantering away.

'No. I'd have missed,' I said. 'You're the stalker.'

'It was a clean shot. He was going for a hind, full of testosterone and adrenalin. He wouldn't have felt a thing.'

The stag was massive. A strong musky smell, not unpleasant, thick and heavy, hung in the air. I stood by his antlers, his majestic head. Ewan poked one of the open eyes with his stick. 'It's best to check. Beautiful, isn't he?'

I knelt and brushed a hand across the warm pelt, matted from rolling in peat hags.

'It's one of those things. You only get close to the beast by killing him.'

He pulled a knife from his knapsack, felt his way along the belly and slid the knife in. Steaming entrails spilled into the heather.

'Gralloching. It'll give the ravens something to eat after we're gone.' He finished the gutting and bound the stag's back legs together with rope from his knapsack.

'I'll get the Argo and we can drive him part-way, then I'll drag him the rest of the way down the hill. We do the butchering down at the lodge. You'll stay here?'

I sat on the heather beside the stag and drank from my flask. I breathed in the musk and the slight sweet smell of the entrails. Flies flew in.

'*Poor old bastard*,' I whispered. '*None of us know when it's coming.*'

In the Land Rover, driving back to Kyle, Ewan said, 'Do you know what the meaning of life is, Dan?'

Of course I didn't.

'For me it's stalking.' He indicated the mountains surrounding us. 'You see all this, the hills and lochs and burns,
more than a hundred square miles of it? It's mine.'

He let out a laugh.

'Of course it's not mine really. But in a way, it is. I walk
it every year. I know where the golden eagles' and the
ravens' nests are. I know the deer. I know its birds, its
plants, where the badgers and foxes and otters are. I know
it better than anyone; better even than the "owner". Stalking gives me that. Gives me life.'

Once, during a calm period of my own life, I went
to a wedding where I sat for a time chatting drunkenly with
a young woman, a stranger to me. I told her what I was
doing with my days just then, and enthused about how
completely contented I was with my lot. I thought she'd
be pleased for me – so many people are just struggling
on – but she wasn't. She was disbelieving, became bitter,
then stomped off. You can keep your contentment, she
implied, and you can shove it. I didn't understand. I
hadn't been crowing, just sharing. Shouldn't we have been
rejoicing?

I envied Ewan, his knowing where he belonged. I hadn't
a clue.

Ewan dropped me off at the island and went to Kyle
to fetch his wife. It was still early afternoon. When they
returned we stood in the sun for a while, gazing down the
loch to the Kintail hills.

'We used to come here when we were kids,' Ewan said. 'We'd sail or row across from Kyle and annoy the lighthouse keepers. They always kept a visitors' book at the top of the lighthouse and when we arrived we had to sign it.'

'Did you ever come here when Gavin Maxwell lived here?' I asked.

Ewan shook his head. 'It was all "Private! Keep Out!"' Ewan's wife said. 'It put a lot of people's backs up.'

I showed them around the island. Looking at the photographs in the Long Room, Ewan's wife said, 'He was always with young boys, Maxwell, wasn't he though?'

'Not so young,' I said. I hadn't quite made up my mind about all that.

That evening I drove over to Skye to see Susan Browning and her husband. ('A pederast!' the husband proclaimed when the subject of Maxwell came up.) I couldn't tell them about the stalking; I knew they'd disapprove. The scent of the stag's pelt lingered on my fingers, like the trace of sex. As we ate dinner, whenever I lifted food to my mouth I could smell it.

Susan told me she'd resigned from the Trust. She was tired and felt she'd done enough. She planned to dedicate more time to her art and gardening. There'd be someone else looking after the visitors' centre and the house lettings when everything reopened at Easter. Susan looked younger that evening, smiling and laughing, and after dinner she became expansive – enthusing about the wildlife that visited her garden, about the blackbird that pecked impatiently at the kitchen window whenever she or her husband were tardy in putting out food for it, about their new life in the Highlands.

'And a decision has been made,' she told me. 'You can stay on the island if you wish. The trustees are very pleased with what you've achieved. But actually,' she added, 'it was so bad before, they couldn't fail to notice a difference.'

There'd been a vote. The Trust still couldn't pay me a salary but grant applications were being prepared. With luck, money would come for renovations and improvements to the visitors' centre and the island, maybe even for salaries. What did I think?

I had savings to last me a year, if I were careful. I sang as my car bounced over the hills back to the island and I slept very little that night, kept awake as I was by possibilities running through my mind.

≈

With no one booked to stay in the cottage until Christmas and the tours finished for the year, it seemed a good time to get on with some major repair work to the house. The bathroom needed replastering and the kitchen and bedrooms repainting. Wind-driven rain had soaked through exterior mortar and brickwork. The plasterboard wall above the gable-end fireplace in the Long Room was bubbled and falling apart; that whole end of the house needed drying out.

I was lying on the sofa in my room when a shadow fell across the book I was reading. Sandy's rosy face loomed large as he put a hand to the half-window door and peered in.

The first thing he said to me was: 'Bit of a playboy, wasn't he, Maxwell? A toff. Liked to play the big man. All those racing cars and Mercs, trips abroad, nice flat in the posh part of London paid for by Mummy. He's not so well remembered round here, not from what I've heard.'

The second thing he said was: 'Oh good, someone with a decent coffee-maker. Cold day, brrr . . .' One of the trustees had talked him into carrying out the repairs to the house. He'd come over to see what needed doing, brrr . . .

'Oh, would you li—?'

'Milk and two sugars'll be fine.'

He sniffed, looked around, studying the contents of my room.

'Treated some people round here very badly, Maxwell did,' Sandy said. 'Always tardy settling his accounts with local tradesmen. Funny bugger, sounds like.'

And Maxwell *was* a funny bugger. I'd read he was neurotic, and manic-depressive, bedevilled. And queer. His attempt at marriage laughably brief, and rather tragic. I suspected that if he liked you or respected you, or could make use of you, he made time for you, otherwise you were nobody. But what did I really know? Only what I'd read in books and surmised. I'd never met the man. My imaginings of Gavin Maxwell's personality traits were just that, imaginings. And we are all forever changing our masks to suit circumstance, busy keeping our other rooms out of sight.

Sandy leant against the sink and swigged his coffee.

'I've never been on the island before.'

'Would you like to have a look around, Sandy?' I said.

'Aye. Please. Always wanted to have a shufti but it's always been like, "Keep Out!" No-one likes that attitude up here. Too English.'

He swilled the last of his coffee and washed up the cup. I followed him out the door.

'How's your little boat?' he asked. 'You hardly ever see a dinghy out and about anymore. Used to be awash with boats, the Hebrides – post boats and passenger ships, ferries where they've now put bridges, fishing boats. Now everyone drives everywhere. Nobody's got any time to dawdle.'

'It's all changed,' I said.

'Almost all.'

I showed Sandy the area behind the cottage where the aviary had been and where the ghosts were said to walk on winter evenings.

'Seen any?'

'Not yet.'

We walked on down the cobbled path.

'They could do so much with this place. That light-house you've got there is the most accessible Stevenson lighthouse in the whole of the British Isles. Its historic importance is phenomenal. But nobody's allowed on the island to visit it.'

'That's not true,' I said, 'The tours—'

'The tours . . . Pah! Not everyone wants a guided tour. Most people just want to visit the lighthouse.'

I disagreed. 'All sorts of people come here. Maxwell fans, otter fans, birdwatchers, local-history buffs, tourists just looking for something to do, and yes, lighthouse enthusiasts, and locals.'

'Well, otters are everywhere up here,' Sandy said. 'As for Maxwell fans . . . such people exist? No. The main focus of the Kyleakin Lighthouse Island Trust should be the Stevenson lighthouse and the story of the lighthouse keepers.'

I'd had similar conversations. Everyone had a view on how the island should be used, skewed by their own inter-ests. Repeat visitors to the island often buttonholed me with a list of things they thought needed improving. Sandy was no different in this respect.

I unlocked the door to the lighthouse and we climbed the stairs to the service room and clambered out onto the balcony. We were sixty feet up, the island spread out beneath us under grey skies, and encircling the island that

360° vista of mountain and sea. A car *kerlumped* over the bridge.

'Living here,' I said, 'it's a twenty-year dream come true.'

'It's a fine place, right enough.'

Sandy ambled out of sight round the balcony. Being up high – up a mountain or a hill, or a lighthouse – calms me, a tonic for my soul. I walked round to join Sandy.

'Look,' he said quietly, 'out there by the green buoy. See it? Swimming this way?'

The otter swam underwater for a time, surfaced, glanced around, dived. The wind blew our scent far away over the sea; the otter had no idea it was being observed. It swam to the base of the lighthouse beneath us and slipped out of the sea to lollop along the rocks before lifting its rump to spraint. Then it slipped back into the sea and swam, porpoising, past the slipway. We stood gripping the railing and peering down into the bay until the otter swam out of view.

'Lovely,' Sandy said. 'I leave mackerel out for one that comes onto the pontoons down by *Ebb 'n Flow*. It doesn't seem to mind the dog, teases him in fact.'

We walked up to the cottage and I showed him what needed doing in the house.

'An old house like this stuck out in the middle of the sea is bound to have damp. Really, that exterior wall wants repointing. It'll need scaffolding, a proper builder's job. But

I'll come across bright and early tomorrow and make a start on the interior.'

A week later he came by to drop off some plasterboard and told me he'd be 'back in a bit'. I didn't see him again for a month.

≈

I visited Sandaig for the second time in 1987. I hadn't been back since the midge-marred 1985 visit with Dara. Now I was eighteen and something of a drug-taker (a phase – most teenagers go through it; my own childhood among commune-dwelling hippies almost necessitated it), and I had the perfect job for a pothead: working the nightshift in a chocolate factory. I could sleep all day, smoke dope in the evenings with my stoner friends and float into the factory for ten. The work was totally mindless, the machines on the shop floor thumped to the rhythm of any pop song I wanted. And as the mists of my evening's toking cleared and the extreme hunger that was a side effect came on, I found myself somewhere better even than a sweetshop – the place where sweets were made. The whole huge building was chock-a-block with chocolate-based product, ice-cold and straight off conveyor belts. I'd clock off at seven and shamble back to the flat to get stoned again before lapsing into a ten- to twelve-hour coma. Fair heaven. The wages were good too.

That chocolate-factory autumn, before the first frosts

began, I filled a Tupperware box with magic mushrooms, which pop up all over the place like pixies at that time of the year. I wanted to trip somewhere formidable, somewhere profound – not slumped in front of a muted TV listening to Pink Floyd, or staggering about in flat fields with inches of mud stuck to the treads of my second-hand paratrooper boots. Sandaig, to my mind, was ideal.

I had bought a little white van. My flatmate Dominic was keen to come along for the ride. He'd never seen Scotland. And I had that boxful of magic mushrooms.

We took the road north out of Norwich and kept going. The North-east was icy cold, a Siberian wind skating in off the North Sea. We headed over the border and on into the glens. At Spean Bridge we stretched our legs and I breathed in once more that mossy, peaty, mildewed air of thousands of acres of freedom. We drove through Glencoe in mist and reached Glenelg long after dark. The pub closed, I drove to the lay-by at Tormor and we slept in the back of the van.

Cold and condensation woke us early. We swallowed forty magic mushrooms each, trekked down to Sandaig and as we approached Maxwell's grave the sun stood clear of a cumulus cloud. I took it as a gesture of welcome. I showed Dominic the cairn beneath the dying rowan.

'I feel a bit sick,' I said.

'Yeah, me too. They're taking effect.'

'Come on. I'll show you the waterfall.'

~

Later, as we were walking across the strand to the islands, rain clouds rolled in from Skye and the wind picked up, snapping short waves onto the beaches. There was that sudden chill to the air, that inhalation before rage.

Dominic looked up at the sky and turned to me.

'*Après moi . . .*' The rain fell in dollops. The only shelter was the old barn. We splashed across the burn and sprinted past Maxwell's grave. Rain and then hailstones thundered down on what remained of the barn's corrugated roof. A filthy disembowelled mattress lay in a corner, and scattered about on the concrete floor were rusting tin cans and the leftovers of a meal of mussels and crab.

Some old tramp must have stayed here. Or who?

We were soaked through and cold.

Dominic slumped down on the cold concrete, stretched out his legs and wrapped himself tight in his khaki ex-army jacket. He pulled out a tobacco tin and set about rolling a cigarette.

'We can get a fire going,' I called out over the bashing on the roof. I took out my wallet, pulled out an old train ticket – from the last trip I'd made to see my family; the till receipt for a book; a library card; a photograph of two of my sisters on a beach in Morocco. I scrunched these things up and placed them on the floor. I plucked stuffing from the mattress, laid some still-dry leaves and twigs on top. But I'd lost a lot of clarity. My sisters, holiday smiles in the sun, looked up at me from the tinder on the floor. They, and home, felt far away, fragmented and unreachable. The rain and hail banged down on the roof like hammer blows while the wind worked its way under it, worrying at the nails that held the corrugated sheeting to the joists, rattling, gnawing, shaking, slamming. We weren't wanted here.

I juggled with matches and set light to the photograph and the ticket but the flame sputtered in the draft and went out. There were only a few matches left. Dominic asked me not to use any more. I asked for a cigarette and sat down opposite him.

'This'll stop soon,' I said. 'Listen. The rain's starting to die down already.'

Dominic took a drag on his cigarette, held out a hand for the tobacco tin. 'Why did we come here?'

I told him the story of Gavin Maxwell and the books he'd written and how they had seized me; how I wished I'd met him and come to live at Sandaig with him in the black-and-white photographed world of his books, exploring the wild coastline in boats, meeting the remarkable people he knew – people like Peter Scott (conservationist, ornithologist, and son of Scott of the Antarctic), James Robertson-Justice (bombastic, charismatic actor and falconer), Wilfred Thesiger (explorer of the Empty Quarter, author of *Arabian Sands*), David Stirling (founder of the SAS), assorted diplomats and spies, journalists, Algerian freedom fighters . . . the sort of people I thought I'd like to meet. How he'd lived adventurously, independently, with aristocratic panache. A risk-taker.

I spoke with enthusiasm and we smoked in an effort to keep warm and I don't think Dominic knew what I was going on about at all. Then the rain stopped and we went outside.

We traipsed through wet rushes and bog myrtle and followed a sheep path up a hill. The ragged clouds lifted and blew away and from the top of the hill we had a fine view across the Sound of Sleat to the great brooding wall of Skye.

I looked away to the boulder where Maxwell's ashes lay. Sandaig was an isolated, intense arena. The silence and the violence and the beauty and ferocity of that place frightened me that day. A heaven can so easily become hell.

We sat on lichened rocks and watched the sea, the Sound like a vast green swimming pool, so calming, the waves marching up the channel towards Kylerhea. We sat on the hill for a long time, the wind gusting through the blackberry bushes and the squall-ravaged, spindly, stunted trees. Then the wind abated a little and the rain returned, spotting hypnotically on the sea below us.

On the way back to the van, the hissing of light rain a live-wire hum in my head, I picked some blackberries to eat and placed one on the boulder for Maxwell's ghost. As we trudged back up the track to the road I tried to picture home and family and friends, but nothing came. There was only the now, and only this. When we reached the van I climbed into my sleeping bag and tried to sleep but sleep was evasive, my mind filling with psychedelic, kaleidoscopic swirls, endlessly turning and merging. Dominic sat in the passenger seat of the van, smoking and silent, and rain clattered gently on the roof.

I visited Sandaig often after that, sometimes hitching up there, driving when I had money to run a car, but always alone; the visits punctuation marks in my life. I swam, and explored the islands and found a way to the upper reaches of the burn, where there are other waterfalls and brighter, less soulful stretches of water. I bought provisions from the Glenelg shop and drank in the now poshed-up pub, even on Sundays – which, over the years, even in the West Highlands, had become less special. I collected wood and cooked my suppers on a fire and retired to my tent when it rained. The weather is always against you at Sandaig, and it is a hard place in which to exist for long under canvas.

Year by year things changed, as Nature reclaimed what was hers. Dara and I had found the rusting remains of the boat trailer of Maxwell's launch, the *Polar Star*, among undergrowth by the wall by the burn. This disintegrated to dust and four perished tyres. The twisted shell of a steel boat hull that I had first spied with a magnifying glass in one of the photographs in *The Otters' Tale* sank further into the beach at the mouth of the burn. The rowan tree by Edal's cairn – the rowan of the curse – rotted to nothing while the larch tree matured. The roof, and later the walls, of the barn where Dominic and I had sheltered collapsed. Only the totems placed around the plaques of the two gravestones remained, forever being blown away by the wind and replaced anew by fans.

And always, on my visits, I found the croft well maintained and trim-looking – whitewashed, telephone line intact, an outside tap, a stack of fish boxes covered and pegged down nearby – but never occupied.

I still didn't quite know why Maxwell appealed to me so strongly. I hadn't pulled the books, or myself, apart then. But he kept coming back to haunt me. It was as though he had his own little shrine in my head. I'd forget about him, move along in life and then, out of nowhere, in a dream (I would be at Sandaig and everyone from the books would be there, except Gavin Maxwell, who was always away, absent, unavailable to see me) or a moment of emptiness, there he'd be, back on my mind again. I guess that is how obsession is.

As I became a little more informed about the ways of the world, I trawled library archives for books and articles about Maxwell. I viewed documentaries about him. I bought signed copies and first editions of his books. And I discovered that Maxwell's friend, Raef Payne ('the Eton schoolmaster from Wales'), rented the croft down at

Sandaig. I sifted telephone directories covering Wales and shook out an address and phone number. I wrote to Raef asking, baldly, if I could stay in the croft sometime. In the directory for the Highlands and Islands I found the phone number of the croft. Once or twice I dialled to listen to it ringing. I pictured the bell by the guttering above the tap, clattering away hundreds of miles away to the north, across the emptiness, disturbing the peace of a still evening, or drowned out by the din of a gale, the roar of the waterfall, the crying of gulls. I couldn't say why I telephoned. No one ever answered. And if someone had ('Glenelg 266. Hello . . . ?'), I'd most likely have slammed down the receiver in a panic.

I continued working at the chocolate factory until I had saved enough money to travel, then quit. I went abroad, stayed out till I was broke, returned to England and found myself another dead-end job, saved up again, went abroad again. Again and again. I hitched across Europe and down through Morocco, sailed into storms and out again. I was like a hamster on a wheel, going nowhere. On a trip to India I smoked so much dope I lost all sense of perspective, and when I got back to England I stopped taking drugs. I went back to school, then on to university to study Arabic.

Douglas Botting's biography, *Gavin Maxwell: A Life*, was published in 1993 and I bought my copy in London on my way out to Damascus, where I was to spend a year as part of my degree course. The biography was a dense, meaty read – revealing, yet misty in parts. (After writing it, Botting said how humbling it had been, seeing another's life mapped out before him – the struggles and triumphs, how a life can be.) I read the book twice over, in my tiny room in Damascus down a little alleyway off The Street Called Straight, oblivious to the heat and dust and the calls to prayer. It fleshed out the bones of the potted biographies I'd read in the Coles' and York's student study guides for *Ring of Bright Water*, and aspects of Maxwell's character hinted at in *Maxwell's Ghost* and *The White Island*. And afterwards I felt less in awe of its subject. When the internet arrived a few years later, I trawled it for mention of Gavin Maxwell and the others in the myth. I moved to London and got a 'proper job' for a time. Then quit.

I fell over, many times, and learnt that it's best to relax into a fall and to roll with it. You get hurt less that way.

≈

Sandy Wood kept his own time. That was obvious. His work schedule was erratic and he'd turn up on the island at any time of the day or night to get on with the repairs.

'When I take a job on,' he told me, 'I like to achieve perfection, and that takes time.' It took him six weeks to replaster one wall and replace a strip of plasterboard in the Long Room, but I didn't mind and I don't think the trustees did either. Especially after Sandy told them he'd decided to do the repairs for free, to help a good cause.

Over those weeks we became friends. Skivvying for Sandy – fetching and carrying while he got on with the more skilled work – allowed me to get to know him, though only a little, for he rarely discussed his past.

'I've got plans, though,' Sandy told me one evening as we sat in my room drinking wine. '*Ebb 'n Flow* is going to make a brilliant sail-training vessel for handicapped kids, disabled and that. She'll be a ketch. The Forestry Commission are saving a couple of good straight sitkas I found for the masts, they're practically giving them to me. I've got most of what I'll need for the conversion stacked up on deck under the tarp, it's just a question now of getting the time and some fine weather to crack on. I really want to get started.' He sipped his wine and stretched out his legs to wiggle wet-socked toes in the warmth coming off the space-heater.

Sandy didn't look in a rush to crack on with anything, let alone his dream boat.

'What'll you tackle first?' I asked, and gagged as I gulped down more of the vile wine Sandy had bought us. ('Lidl's cheapest!' he'd said proudly when he'd handed me the bottle.)

'Rip out all the old fishing gear – the derrick, net-shooter, drum, all that – and sell it for a packet to a scrappy I know.'

These were huge, hefty, industrial-sized pieces of cast iron that would need cutting from the deck with an acetylene torch and craned onto a lorry. It was questionable whether Fisherman's Wharf would be able to take the weight of a lorry, a crane and all the scrap.

'After that the wheelhouse'll go. Then I can start on the decks.'

'*Ebb 'n Flow* is a dog,' I said. *In vino veritas.*

Since my first tipsy visit to Sandy's boat I'd gone there again, in daylight, and although he'd never allowed me below decks, I'd managed a peek into the wheelhouse. It was overflowing with junk, just as the decks were piled with junk, or what looked like junk to me. I told him so.

'Oh, but it's all useful stuff,' Sandy assured me, pulling steaming socks away from the heater. 'I've been collecting since I bought *Ebb 'n Flow* a couple of years back. There're skips all over these isles just filled to the gills with plunder. People chuck out any old thing these days. It's a crime. Just last month I got a whole zinc kitchen unit they were throwing away at the youth hostel. It'll be perfect for the galley and shower unit. Cost a fortune new, it would.'

'*Ebb 'n Flow* will never be seaworthy,' I said. 'Her engines are shot, her hull's a sponge. She's sinking as we speak. And some of that timber you've got under the tarpaulin is riddled with woodworm. The generator I saw looks like it's been pulled out of the sea. It's all corroded. There're barnacles on it. Tow her to a beach and set her on fire, Sandy. Start again. Buy something that's worth something.'

Sandy shook his head.

'It's all good stuff. I'll need it when I convert the boat.'

But I'd seen this before. The father of one of my sisters (my family tree is exceedingly complicated and too multi-faceted (and -fathered) to go into here) had the same illness – hoarding, the need to surround oneself with piles of possessions, stuff, useful and duff. It was more than being 'a collector', or the inability to say no to a bargain. The accumulation of other people's cast-offs filled empty days. Last month's finds were soon buried beneath this month's treasures, with everything getting compacted into a stew of decomposing, disintegrating, moth-eaten, forgotten-about, now-where-did-I-put-it crap.

'Well, if you need a hand with the conversion, I'm keen to help,' I said. 'It'd be good to learn boat building.'

Sandy nodded enthusiastically, 'Once she's converted to sail, after a few seasons with the sail-training, I'm going to take her down to New Zealand. It's a wonderful country.'

Sandy had never been to New Zealand, never been abroad. He was, I reckoned, in his late fifties, although when I'd asked him his age he'd dodged the question, as he dodged any enquiry into his past.

'Well, how old are *you*?' he'd asked me instead.

'Thirty-six.'

'So'm I.'

'Come off it, Sandy,' I'd said. 'I reckon you're . . . fifty-eight, maybe fifty-four . . .'

But Sandy had just smiled and changed the subject.

'When are you starting work on *Ebb 'n Flow*?' I asked, pouring more poison into his glass.

'I have to find a lock-up somewhere to store all the gear off the decks. It needs to be a very secure place though. Some of the gear is very valuable.'

I couldn't believe anyone else would ever want any of it.

'They'll take anything round here,' Sandy said. 'I had some bits taken the other night, bits of wood and that. I know who it was.' He frowned. 'Useful bits I was saving. They'd have been just right for shelving, and making bunk beds in the cabins.'

Months later I was still trying to chivvy him along.

'I've got almost everything I need now,' he'd tell me, 'I just need a place to store it so I can clear the decks, a lock-up or a garage in the village . . . has to be nearby though . . . otherwise it'll take months just moving it off the boat.'

'And . . . ?'

'I've asked around, but there's nothing going.'

And there never was. Sandy slept with his dog somewhere down in the hold of his sinking, rotting dream, growing older, freewheeling, finding small-scale projects to fill his days; surrounding himself with jetsam, and waiting, just until he found the perfect place to store his stuff so he could clear the decks and begin. One day, I thought, they'll find him dead in the bilge of his dream with his dog standing guard over all that crap. Sandy Wood was a kind, lonely man. He was my friend, and he taught me to sail.

Around the time Sandy finally completed the work on the cottage (and Sandy's idea of 'achieving perfection' left me scratching my head), the villages started to go into what felt like hibernation. Traffic over the bridge dwindled, coach parties tailed off and the holidaymakers faded away. Yachts no longer came nodding past the island. The Wednesday Workcrew was suspended. The villagers appeared tranquil, prepared for the long winter ahead, their work done, the money brought in. Autumn is a short season in the Highlands.

I spent weekdays making bird boxes to put up in the spring, repairing the weather-tortured bench in front of the house, clearing an area near Teko's memorial where the lighthouse keepers' wives had once hung their washing. I did some minor repair-work to the lighthouse and the lighthouse shed. When the weather was very bad I worked in the bothy on my book. I hauled my dinghy high up the slipway and tied it down, secure I hoped from raging winter gales. And in the evenings I reread Gavin Maxwell's books, and books about Gavin Maxwell.

≈

Gavin, the last of his mother's brood, was born on 15 July 1914.

Gavin's father, Aymer, was a Maxwell of Monreith – a baronetcy in Galloway; Gavin's mother, Lady Mary, was a daughter of the seventh Duke of Northumberland. Both families were adherents of the Catholic Apostolic Church, believing in the imminence of the Second Coming and the restoration of the twelve apostles. Gavin's delivery hadn't been straightforward, and it left him with five strawberry birthmarks down the inside of his right forearm and a predisposition to ailments and sickness. Three months after Gavin was born, in October 1914, his father was killed in a German artillery barrage in Antwerp. It wasn't so much that Gavin *lost* a father; in truth he never knew one. Lady Mary never remarried and brought up her four children alone, with the aid of attendant servants, tutors, and her very high-powered family.

Lady Mary and her children (a girl and three boys) moved between the House of Elrig on the Wigtownshire moors and family-owned properties in England. The Maxwells weren't royalty, but weren't far removed. Gavin and his siblings were brought up at a time when social and class mobility was practically nil. Class rules forbade fraternization (i.e. playing) with local tykes. You had to stick with your own kind. So you were left to wander the big empty parklands, with often only your pets and extended family for company. Such an isolated childhood isn't the best training for the social minefields beyond the lodge gates.

In 1924, at the age of ten, after being taught by a series of private tutors, Gavin was sent to prep schools (he attended three) and four years later went on to public school (Stowe). Vignettes from this time* may help you to envisage this child: a senior boy at a prep school advising Gavin, 'You've got to learn to be like other people'; a head-master's report on Gavin while he was at Stowe:

> [Gavin] appears utterly incapable of any form of con-centration. Gavin's manner suggests the most perfect indifference to what is going on, and he has quite definitely a vein of indolence in him.

A Stowe contemporary remembered him as 'always looking dreamily out of the window or else sketching in his note-book,' and added: 'out of a form of about thirty boys Gavin was invariably twenty-seventh to thirtieth in every subject every term.'

Another described him as 'just all screwed up'.

Gavin was always away in his head somewhere else, and by his own account made few friends while at school. He was more interested in collecting and looking after the semi-tamed wild animals that Stowe allowed boys to keep. Then, on his sixteenth birthday, Gavin collapsed

---

* Many more can be found in Douglas Botting's biography.

with severe internal bleeding (later diagnosed as Henoch-Schönlein purpura). He left the school grounds in an ambulance and was to spend the best part of a year convalescing, isolated at home with his mother and sister, and often bedridden for fear that movement would set off the bleeding again. Anthony Dickins, Maxwell's friend at Stowe and afterwards, opined in an essay he wrote for *London Magazine* that this 'reduction to a state of almost total physical weakness and dependence' acted like a trauma on Gavin's psyche:

> so that one part of his psyche remained, like a gramophone needle in a rut, at an early teenage stage of development, while other parts continued developing normally. It was as if one part of him were constantly seeking a return to complete the missing portion of the story that had ended so abruptly.

And there is a theory that writers (in my view some, but by no means all) are formed from similar protracted and enforced breaks in the routines of their formative years; an exile from the world that expands beyond the norm the interior imaginative life of the individual. And creative writing, especially autobiographical writing (which Maxwell excelled at), is often about imposing order on the past, a reliving and retelling of life as it should have been and not necessarily as it was.

Once recovered, and perfectly naturally for a member

of the huntin', shootin' and fishin' set, Gavin took up, in a big way, stalking, game shooting and wildfowling. In the spring of 1933, after attending a crammer, he went to Hertford College, Oxford to study Estate Management. Being not wildly interested in estate management as a subject (or career), Maxwell attended lectures on zoology, medicine and art outwith his own school of studies. His peers considered him rather aloof, 'raffish and well-heeled' (he roared around in a Bentley). He graduated in 1937, with a third-class degree.

Through the law of primogeniture – the system where-by the eldest son inherits all – Gavin's eldest brother, Aymer, would inherit the Monreith estate, which left Gavin casting around for 'something to do'.

He worked for a year as a travelling salesman for a small agricultural firm in Hereford. Over the summers of 1938 and 1939, taking up a suggestion by fellow wildfowler (and future conservationist and founder of the Wildfowl and Wetlands Trust at Slimbridge), Peter Scott, Maxwell went to Finnmark in Norwegian Lapland to photograph and study the Steller's eider duck. Maxwell was stuck on becoming an explorer – to travel to remote places, have adventures and then write about them. A good plan, but he lacked the constitution, both mentally and physically (he was plagued by ill-health all his life).

Maxwell joined the Scots Guards in August 1939. Health problems (a duodenal ulcer, an enlarged heart, beside others) precluded him from active service. He found his way into SOE – the Special Operations Executive – a clandestine 'secret army' established by Churchill in 1940 to prepare agents for sabotage, espionage, reconnaissance and resistance operations behind enemy lines.

During World War II, movement north of the Caledonian Canal was restricted. It was a secret country up there. Twenty-five thousand commandos passed through the basic-training centre at Achnacarry House near Spean Bridge. Some of the paramilitary and commando training of SOE agents took place in requisitioned country houses and shooting lodges around Arisaig. Many SOE agents came from the countries that were under Nazi occupation. Each nationality was billeted at a different base: among others, the French at Moeble Lodge, Czechs at Garramor House, Poles at Camusdarach, Belgians at Rhubana Lodge and Norwegians at Glaschoille House on Knoydart. About 3,000 SOE agents trained at these lodges in close combat, fieldcraft, explosives and demolition, and signalling. Then they were sent into Axis territory, where many met their deaths.

Maxwell, with a facility with guns and fieldcraft learnt whilst out stalking, wildfowling and on grouse moors, became a small-arms and fieldcraft instructor.

SOE was meritocratic – it didn't matter who you were, who you knew or where you schooled; safe-cracking, burglary and forgery being as important to the cause as straight soldiering. Maxwell's colleagues were an eclectic, adventurous bunch. He was free of the usual strictures of forces life. He set up home where he wished and kept a lobster boat and a motorcycle. He had a good war.

Now, I realize that biographers sometimes fall prey to the same sin of omission as some statisticians – plucking facts to fit their purpose – but I would like to include here the words of a former SOE colleague of Maxwell's:

> [Gavin] was very witty, very entertaining, very well-bred; and though he could be irritable and prickly, he was usually great to be with and cheered people up a lot.
>
> He was also quite the most neurotic person I have ever met in my life.*

An SOE psychiatrist profiled Maxwell as having a personality perpetually at war with itself, experiencing conflicting emotions and contradictory attitudes. I'm no shrink, but add to this diagnosis Maxwell's manic-depressive tendencies and the emotional trauma of his year-long convalescence and you've a recipe, I reckon, for an artistic, impossible personality.

Before the war had been played out, the SOE training camps were run down. Maxwell was invalided out in November 1944, with the rank of Major. During the

---

* Botting, p. 61.

summer of 1943 Maxwell had visited Soay – a small isle off Skye – and decided to buy it, planning to earn interest on his investment from feu-duties (land rent) and fishing rights. And by chance he found a future occupation – hunting basking sharks.

Basking sharks are massive – thirty feet and more in length – and the oil in their liver was a valuable commodity once, used in the production of cosmetics and much else. Gavin Maxwell wasn't the first or the last adventurer to go chasing these behemoths around the Hebrides (and Anthony Watkins and Patrick Fitzgerald O'Connor also wrote books about doing so). Maxwell bought boats, took on Tex Geddes (a fellow SOE instructor – of explosives and boat-handling) and others, and employed the Soay islanders at the processing plant he had built on the island.

The story of Soay Shark Fisheries has been recounted by Maxwell himself in *Harpoon at a Venture*. It is a well-written book about a short story. By the spring of 1948, after only three seasons, the basking shark venture was over and Maxwell had lost almost all of his capital. He was thirty-four years old.

Retreating to Monreith, broke and, not surprisingly, depressed, Maxwell picked himself up and embarked on a new scheme (all his life his head was full of schemes) – to transform himself into a society portrait painter. Painting, illustration, art, had always been hobbies. He had formidable social connections, access to stately drawing rooms throughout the land. He took instruction and willed himself into his new role, but as Kathleen Raine was to write in a memoir, 'his paintings were extremely conventional', and he knew it.

Around this time Maxwell was offered the lease of the house at Sandaig by his friend and Oxford contemporary Anthony Wills (later Lord Dulverton) – of Wills tobacco and cigarettes – who had recently bought the Eilanreach estate, on which Sandaig lies.

Maxwell moved to London, got a few commissions for portraits, and tried to find his way again. He was reliant financially now on his mother and his brother Aymer (who had by this time inherited Monreith and the baronetcy). The collapse of a romantic relationship pulled a final rug from beneath his feet and left him floored. He suffered a nervous breakdown.

The (very sporting) psychiatrist (a Harley Street practitioner, naturally) who treated Maxwell for depression at this time advised him that 'the best thing to do if you feel like killing yourself is to go off and do something really dangerous.' So Maxwell took to competitive driving, hurling his 3.5-litre Rolls Bentley around the racetracks of Silverstone and Goodwood.

In August 1949, at a house in Chelsea, Gavin Maxwell was introduced to Kathleen Raine.

Four

Staying In

Before I go forward I'd like to take you back, just for a short while, to when I was nineteen, before Botting's excellent biography appeared and when I still knew so little. For I met Raef Payne, Maxwell's great friend and the renter of the croft at Sandaig, that September of 1988, at his house, which wasn't in Wales as I've written, but on the outskirts of the partisan village of Llanymynech, which keeps a foot in both camps, sited as it is on the England–Wales border.

I'd hitched across England and Wales to southern Ireland and was on my way back to Norfolk. Eire in those pre-EU days was one of the poorest nations in Western Europe, made up of hospitable and talkative people. I was given lifts by farmers driving their pigs to market and beckoned in by mothers taking carloads of kids to school. A very drunken man on his way home from an afternoon's drinking stopped his car for me and complained as we swerved along on our way about the impossibly high car-insurance premiums in Eire. 'They say it is due,' he told me, 'to the high number of motor accidents that occur, inexplicably, on our quiet rural roads. I *can't* under-stand it.'

Along the coast roads of south-west Ireland my path kept crossing with that of a fellow hitcher called James, a New Yorker. He seemed eternally tired. We ended up lift-sharing – the one already moving along in a vehicle getting his 'driver' to stop for the other if he was seen standing on the side of the road ahead. James kept falling asleep in the vehicles that picked him up. 'Moving hotels,' he called them.

On my way to Dublin to catch the ferry home to Eng-land, leaving the charmless industrial town of Limerick, I walked backwards, with a raised thumb, for miles. The rain that day was vile. Desperate for a lift, as a motorist advanced towards me I fell to my knees and held up my hands in prayer. The car stopped and I got in.

The driver of the car was an Englishwoman in her thirties. A toddler was strapped into a child's seat. I asked the woman what she was doing in Ireland and she told me the following story:

'I originally came to live in Ireland with a man from County Clare I'd met in London, where I'd been working. I'd fallen for his charm and the blarney and he persuaded me to come back with him to Ireland. But our love fell apart, as so many couples' love does, and eventually I left him. We hadn't been together long enough to talk babies. I think I was afraid of settling down and so was he.

'I got my own flat in Limerick City and a receptionist job at the Bauxite factory down on the Shannon Estuary. It was undemanding work, an undemanding life really. But the constant rain got me down and I didn't feel at home among the Irish, however pleasant and welcoming they may be. I missed home.

'My dad's an engineer and at that time he and my mum lived in Zaire, in Africa, where he was working on water projects. I saved money, packed in the job and the flat and flew out to stay with them. I wanted sun and a total change of atmosphere and to be among people who knew me well and loved me. I thought I'd stay in Africa six months or so, relax a bit, sort out some kind of long-term career plan, then go back to the UK.

'A week after I arrived I met a metallurgist, Paul. We fell in love, got married and ended up staying in Zaire seven years. Last year Paul got offered a job with perks we couldn't refuse, at the Bauxite factory back here on the Shannon Estuary. I'm very pleased to be back. And it felt like coming home. This feels like home.

'The Bauxite factory, Limerick, Ireland, the Irish: they're the same as when I left seven years ago, they've hardly changed at all. It's not about place, or work, or the people around you. Do you see what I mean?'

The ferry from Dublin docked in Holyhead after midnight and I was one of the last foot passengers shooed out into the cold dread night. It was too late to hitch and I couldn't face unpacking my tent so I found a roundabout outside town and lay on the springy turf to snooze until dawn. It started to rain. I still couldn't face unpacking my tent so trudged off and found shelter under a boat at the yacht club. At first light I walked back to the road and stuck out my thumb.

I dozed through most of the lifts that morning – catnapping my way through Wales – and awoke in late afternoon near Llanymynech. I got the driver to drop me off and after a short walk came to the driveway of a modest Georgian country house. A sign on the gate stated that members of the Caravan Club were welcomed. An ideal excuse for an introduction presented itself to my mind. I walked up the driveway. A grey-haired man of about sixty was weeding a flowerbed.

'Hello,' I said, 'I saw the sign and wondered if you might have somewhere I could pitch a tent for the night.' Then for some reason (guilelessness?), I immediately blew my cover: 'Are you Raef Payne?'

'I am indeed,' the man said and straightened up to take me in. 'I'm afraid we've nowhere for tents.' He paused. I'd been hitching, and camping beside smoky fires, for a week. I didn't look very tidy. 'But I could offer you a bed for the night and a bath, if that would be of any use to you.'

I nodded and followed Raef into the hall. Introduction effected, I forgot about the subterfuge; I was tired. 'I wrote to you once,' I blurted out to his back, 'about renting the croft at Sandaig.'

'Aha!' Raef said. He turned and smiled delightedly. 'Yes, I remember. I'm sorry I never replied,' and he let me down gently, telling me the Eilanreach Estate allowed him the use of the croft on the condition that he only used it himself.

'And it's extremely basic inside. You'd do better to rent one of the other houses on the estate. There's even Tormor, up on the road above Sandaig.'

But fixated as I was on Sandaig, none of the others would do.

Raef offered me a drink and showed me his house. In his study a high bookcase was crammed with Maxwell's books – paperbacks, hardbacks, foreign editions. Maxwell's portrait, painted in oils by Raef, hung on a wall.

He had spent almost the whole of his life at Eton – as scholarship boy, as a classics master and seventeen years as a house master. Now he was retired, he told me, 'on gardening leave'.

On the wall of the room where I was to sleep was a 'Spy' cartoon of Maxwell's grandfather, Sir Herbert Maxwell. I'd seen it in a photograph of the Sandaig sitting room in *Raven Seek Thy Brother*.

'A mock-up,' Raef said. 'The BBC had it made for a

documentary they did about Gavin. All that Latin you see there beside the portrait – made-up gibberish. The original, you see, was destroyed in the Sandaig fire.'

Almost nothing had been saved from the flames: the manuscript of *Raven Seek Thy Brother* – the book Maxwell was working on, a couple of guns and Teko, little else.

Maxwell and Andrew Scot – the last-but-one otter boy – spent the next few months living in Raef's croft, before moving to the cottage on Kyleakin Lighthouse Island. The cause of the fire was never determined. And owing to a lapsed policy nothing was insured.

'It was a tragedy,' Raef said at dinner that evening, 'and I think it destroyed Gavin. He lost everything. When something like that happens, when everything you own is so violently wrested away from you, it takes a great deal of strength to begin again. And by then Gavin was sick, although none of us knew it.'

At dinner, Raef and I were joined by a man who lived in an annexe of the house. After dinner the man disappeared. Raef lit a fire in the sitting room and we drank wine and talked about India, a country, Raef told me, that Gavin had always planned to visit.

'He had so many plans,' I remember Raef sighing, 'so many schemes, but never any money. He was always short.'

Raef fetched a photograph album, but my hopes of being shown pictures of Maxwell and the boys at Sandaig quickly faded when I was shown holiday snaps of Raef and a friend ambling in the avenues of Tangier, a trip to China, scenes from the Djemaa el-Fnaa in Marrakesh.

'It's a shame you never met Gavin,' Raef said at one point. 'He'd have liked you.'

We finished the bottle of wine and I went to my room. On closing the door I wondered for a moment if I ought to lodge a chair under the doorknob. But Raef was no Uncle Monty.

In the morning, after breakfast, Raef showed me a studio that Jimmy Watt had converted for him from the stable block.

'Did Jimmy become a builder then?' I asked.

'More of a renovator, really.' Jimmy was like a younger brother to Raef, and it was Jimmy who looked after the croft at Sandaig, kept it spruce and stocked with fish boxes for firewood.

'Jimmy rather prefers to remain in the background. He was never comfortable with Gavin putting him in his books.'

Raef and Jimmy Watt were still directors of the company that had been set up to manage Maxwell's affairs. They were his literary executors and looked after his interests, and they were protective of his reputation.

'Gavin liked to pretend he was a recluse,' Raef said, 'but he craved company. He liked to talk – he was a brilliant conversationalist. He was no good when left for too long on his own.'

As I was preparing to leave, signing the visitors' book, visualizing the long road-trip ahead, Raef said to me, 'I expect you'd like to write Gavin's biography, wouldn't you?'

I squirmed. 'Perhaps,' I said, 'One day.'

'Writers are like magpies. Incurable thieves.'

He drove me to the outskirts of the village and dropped me off by the main road, where I stood a better chance of hitching a lift.

'We could meet at Sandaig,' Raef suggested, 'next year. You could use the croft to cook in when the weather turns bad. I go in April because there are hardly any midges or visitors then. I like to be alone there and remember how it was in the early days, when Gavin and the boys and the otters were there. You'd be good company.'

'Perhaps,' I said.

But we never did meet down at Sandaig. The lines of our lives never converged again. Raef Payne died in 2001. I have his obituary here beside me as I write.

I stood by the roadside for a quarter of an hour that day. A decommissioned, disintegrating ambulance slowed to a stop beside me. Its driver was a science undergraduate travelling back to university. He had twists of cream lavatory paper stuffed up his nostrils.

'Got uh gold,' he intoned when I enquired, 'Stops ze vlow.'

≈

November. Copper-coloured pine needles lined the glistening, flooded winter roads. Hotel and guesthouse staff were laid off till Easter, restaurant- and cafe-owners shut up shop. The pavements and beaches lacked the strolling couples of the summer months; I missed the sound of voices drifting across water.

The seals were gone now, gone to the breeding grounds, but eider ducks – big, colourful sea ducks – *ooh-oohing*, came to paddle and drift around the island, and on windless days the silence would be broken by splashings as they ran heavily along the surface of the sea, wings flapping wildly to get airborne. On these days of glass-calm seas, chaffinches and dunnocks and robins emerged from their hiding places to preen and feed and sing. Flocks of redwing on their way south landed to strip the island's rowan trees of berries, then flew on. A *ménage à trois* of red-breasted mergansers took up residence in East Bay, and long-legged curlews and redshanks visited the shoreline. Determined turnstones scuttled and prodded the seaweed. Staggered Vs of geese made their hauntingly voiced way over the island. I'd hear their honking and stand in the doorway and look up and high, high, overhead . . . the hounds of heaven, back from their summer feeding grounds in the Arctic, heading south-east down the loch.

Mice, drawn to the warmth of the cottage, scritch-scratched an increasingly well-worn path up the plasterboard walls to the roof space. They stripped foam lagging from water pipes to make nests. At night in bed I could hear them clomping about. Sometimes they came into my room. They took the poison I left for them, but they didn't die. I set mousetraps and removed the dead.

The winds blew and keened and howled and wooed down the chimneys. The winds made window panes shudder and road signs clatter and fall. A dash of colour – tiny yellow flowers – spilled out of the gorse that grew on the bank by the bridge, and stayed. By four o'clock in the afternoon it was dark. I ordered up quantities of books from the library in Kyle and lay on my sofa and read. Through the half-windowed door I could see the warm orange glow of houselights across the water where, during the day, I might watch long green waves surf past the island, blown down the loch by a force-9 come in from the west. And on windless nights, sometimes, I'd hear the walls of the house flake and fall behind the sheets of plaster-board that lined them.

On fine days I went hiking in the Cuillins and explored the north and the east. Nearby community centres and village halls hosted ceilidhs and put on plays; travelling shows and exhibitions visited. The West Ross Field Club, the Scottish Wildlife Trust and the Kyleakin Lighthouse Island Trust organized monthly lectures, where slides were shown and a talk given to an intimate audience of mainly elderly incomers. There were talks on 'Traditional Medicine', 'The Birds of Skye', 'Our Viking Heritage',

'Dolphins, Porpoises and other Cetaceans of the Hebrides', 'Butterflies and Moths', 'Toadstools', 'Wildlife Photography', 'Deer', 'The West Highland Seashore', 'Remarkable Trees' . . . After, we loudly applauded. Then the scraping of chairs on lino would segue into the clinking of cups on saucers and the murmur of a little light networking. Always the same faces: a preponderance of incomers, a smattering of locals, and me – always the youngest there, by about twenty years.

Over the summer and autumn I'd remained remote, and had been a rare visitor to the pubs in the villages. I shared the paranoia that many English feel when they move to Celtic lands. We know we're not really wanted. The English have historical 'previous': think of the Highland Clearances or the Welsh Not,* think absentee landlords and Famine. The English have been oppressors and usurpers, loud, crass and bullying; an occupying, colonial force. English imperialism and heavy-handedness, the injustices of the past, still cause Celtic eyes to narrow, mouths to move, and men to bare their teeth. The Scots, the Welsh and the Irish don't forget, unlike us English, who've moved on.

---

* A punishment used in some schools in Wales, between the eighteenth and early twentieth centuries, to dissuade the speaking of Welsh. A stick or token – the 'Welsh Not' – was handed to any child caught speaking Welsh in class. The 'Not' could then be passed on to another child caught, or informed on for, speaking Welsh. The child wearing the 'Not' at the end of the school day would be punished.

But sometimes I'd visit the pubs, to sit at a table, alone but in company, to catch village gossip or listen to the SAS boys up on manoeuvres speaking in code – their every other word an acronym; eavesdropping on the lives of others, while outside the rain beat down on washed-clean streets, and white gulls stood grumpy on black chimneypots.

On nightly meanders around the island before bed I'd look west, where across miles of black water, behind the lump of the Isle of Raasay, the amber street lights of the only sizeable town within sixty miles – Portree – licked the sky like a flame. By Kyle of Lochalsh, the Black Isle beacons blinked black–white and the harbour lights pulsed red–green. The lights on the bridge twinkled and flashed, silently and continuously, reflected in the waters of Light-house Bay, projected onto the phallic white screen of the lighthouse, smeared when I blinked through a gauze of fine slanting rain.

One night,

14 November 2005

Back from a walk around the island. The night is dry and cold after three days of continuous heavy rain. The strong winds have blown the storm clouds north. Now there is no wind. A clear, cloudless night, the stars bright above me in the undiluted dark-ness. A full moon paints the paths bright white. Just seen a barn owl ghost under the bridge and alight on a girder to pluck at something in its talons. Hardly a sound but the soft lapping of

the loch on the shore, the occasional thrum of a ship or a navy
tug passing the island under the bridge and away out to sea. I
stand outside the door of my room on this lonely knocked-about
almost-isle, drinking down a view I know I will never possess
again.

I would go to bed and be woken by a fierce drumming
of rain on the Velux window above my bed.

During the long winter evenings, when there were no
guests staying, I'd open all the interior doors of the cottage
and get a fire blazing in the Long Room grate. With
Sandy's help I'd removed the cap on the chimney above
the fireplace. Marcus and I had collected a lot of driftwood
on our beach-cleaning circumnavigations, and there was
always more along the shoreline after gales and spring
tides. I'd sit long on Maxwell's old sofa in the Long Room,
occasionally in the company of Sandy, but mostly alone,
feeding logs into the fire and watching shadows play
across the curtains and walls, across Raef Payne's portrait
of his friend, across Maxwell's furniture and pictures, his
wall-hangings and desk; across his stuff. I'd grow wistful
and wonder about the author of those books on the shelf
beside me, reflect on the lighthouse keepers and the other
ghosts who'd sat by a fire in that room before me. The fire
drew well in the grate, the driftwood crackled and snapped,
warming the house and drawing damp from the walls. But

those fireside cogitations on Maxwell and his world made
no sense, not really.

I was attempting to psychoanalyse a dead man who
lived during a time I had never known. It is a rare thing to
be able to fathom one's own motives; attempting to understand those of a long-dead stranger is madness. The sum
of a person can never be known fully by another. Everyone
hides wounds under skin-coloured patches and a life isn't
linear but a series of blind corners – L-shaped. We never
know what's coming. Think of that stag. Think back to
being ten, or twenty-three or fifty, and what came after.
You've travelled so far to where you are now from where
you were then. How did you come to be holding these
words of mine in your hands, meet the people you now
know, do the job that you do? Was there, is there, really any
plan?

≈

I'd read about the ghosts that are said to haunt the island.
Maxwell never personally experienced ghostly activity
there, but Richard Frere, who lived on the island while
converting the lighthouse keepers' cottages for Maxwell,
wrote a lot about the phenomenon he called 'the time-
locked army'. Joyce, the daughter of the last lighthouse
keeper and today the mother of a grown-up daughter, has
heard many stories about the island's ghosts. Every light-

house keeper who ever lived on the island had stories to tell: of furtive whisperings in an unknown tongue, the sound of steel being dragged across stone, apparitions, presences.

I'd meet strangers who'd say with a glint in their eye, 'Oh! You're living out *there*, are you? You do *know* the island's haunted?' They'd watch me closely, waiting for a flicker of fear. I didn't tell guests in the cottage about the rumours of ghosts but several experienced strange happenings: a shadowy figure passing along the corridor at the back of the cottage, a TV in an empty room switching itself on, the smell of cigarette-smoke in a bedroom when no one in the house smoked, a wraithlike presence by the Long Room fireplace, Gaelic mutterings in the lighthouse. A conservator who came to stay was awoken one night by the *Ptsszz* sound you hear when someone cracks the cap off a bottle of beer, the smacking of lips, gulping sounds and a long, thirst-quenched 'Aahhhh!' The conservator was alone in the house that night; I was away. When I returned to the island he rushed up to ask what I thought. He was truly spooked.

I don't believe in ghosts any more. I'd like to but I can't. Walking back one night from a pub in Kyleakin I noticed a light shining in the window of the Long Room. I knew for sure I'd switched off all the lights before leaving the cottage. I may have been tipsy, but I wasn't drunk. Maxwell had reported stories of similar unexpected lights being seen around the island and house. I looked for an explanation and found it easily enough. That ghostly light was the reflection of a streetlight on the Kyleakin road, cast across the water to the window of the house.

I heard strange sounds all the time on the island, but like the light in the window they were explicable: bramble tendrils clawed each other and scratched against rock and tap-tapped on window panes, mice moved about in the roof; the creaking I'd hear on hot days wasn't the approach of an arthritic-kneed ancient, but the black plastic guttering expanding in the heat of the sun. And it was the wind, not the ghostly mutterings of the Gael and the Viking undead, that whispered and hissed as it swept through dried stalks of bracken.

I have another theory about the island's ghostly mutterings. Sound travels. At the back of the house there's a curved buttress of rock, which resembles a little those concrete dishes – 'sound mirrors' – that in the 1930s were erected along the coast of Britain as early warning devices. Before the advent of radar, these acoustic 'listening ears' were very good at capturing the drone of approaching aeroplanes.

The windows of the bedrooms and bathroom of the cottage face this buttress. My theory is that on still days the voices and vehicles of Kyle and Kyleakin carry over the water and reverberate off the buttress to set up the whispered murmurings of the time-locked army.

Or perhaps it is more esoteric than that. I've come across the website of the artist Tom Newton, who writes:

Hendersen's Bridge, built in the nineteenth century from the stone remains of croft dwellings and meeting houses on the Hebridean island of Raasay, has for generations been reputed to emit the sounds of human voices and dogs barking: a ghostly bridge. Science has proved, however, that the high iron-ore content in the stones of the bridge structure has, by way of a natural magnetic recording, trapped these sounds within, with no sense of time. When atmospheric conditions are favourable, these sounds are released, causing this strange phenomenon to occur.

As for the apparitions – Joyce, the last lighthouse keeper's daughter, likes to blame the fumes from the Brasso with which the keepers polished the rails and fittings of the lighthouse. Failing eyesight unchecked by spectacles? Mental fatigue from weeks of watch-keeping? Too much whisky?

A Principal lighthouse keeper, William Mowatt, died on the island in February 1893. The Northern Lighthouse Board Register does not record whether William fell from the tower or drowned while out in a boat collecting stores or fishing, or from natural causes. William is the only person to have died on the island since the first lighthouse keeper stepped ashore in 1855. Before that time, we'll never know . . .

The stories filter down, the ghostly goings-on go on.

≈

The oil baron John D. Rockefeller, at one time the richest man in the world, once expounded on the secret of success. It is simple, he stated. Get up early, work late – and strike oil. I wasn't doing any of these things.

Gavin Maxwell struck oil, metaphorically speaking, in 1960 with *Ring of Bright Water*, and it took the writing of four books and many early mornings and late nights to get him there.

After moving to London in 1949, Maxwell mixed with fellow aristocrats, ex-SOE colleagues and, increasingly, denizens of the bohemian half-light of post-war literary London. Maxwell's friend from Stowe days, Anthony Dickins, introduced him to Meary James Thurairajah Tambimuttu – 'Tambi', a poetry publisher and impresario and habitué of the pubs and between-hours drinking clubs around Soho and Fitzrovia. Tambi and Dickins had founded a magazine, *Poetry London*, before the War, which later morphed into a publishing house, Editions Poetry London. Tambi had published Kathleen Raine's first two collections of poetry and he viewed Raine as one of his stars. He collected talent, lived in a state of chaos and great enthusiasms, and was an astute judge of literary ability.

(The propensity to sport a beret, smoke Gauloises and lounge louche in the saloon bar of the Poets' Pub is one thing, creative imagination and a workmanlike attitude quite another. And I should know, I've been in that pub striking poses for years.)

On hearing that Maxwell was trying to make a go of it as a portraitist, Tambi encouraged him to paint a series of portraits of literary figures of the day and hold an exhibition to drum up future commissions. To this end he took Maxwell round to meet Kathleen Raine at her house in Chelsea.

Raine was well known and respected in the London literary circle. She was forty-one years old, twice married, with two children at boarding school. Maxwell was thirty-five, not much interested in women, coming out of a depression caused by the collapse of both the shark-fishing venture and a relationship, and adrift. Later Raine was to write in her autobiography, *The Lion's Mouth*: 'It was as if he sought me out, he who seemed to need me; for at that time I was strong, he was weak; I was happy, he wretched; my life had achieved some sort of stability, his was in ruins.'

From this fateful meeting a friendship emerged through a shared love of poetry, and of Northumberland, where they had both spent time as children. It was never an easy friendship, and romantically one-sided. Raine fell for Maxwell in a big way, but Maxwell could never return her feelings. And like children, Maxwell and Raine quarrelled periodically, patched things up, quarrelled again. And at the time of that first meeting, Maxwell did indeed need Raine – to help him break into the literary establishment and get published, and later to look after his first otter, Mij.

Maxwell began to write poetry, and a couple of his poems, through Raine's influence (or at least, introduction) were published in the *New Statesman* magazine in 1950. In the summer of 1950 Maxwell travelled up to Sandaig and with his comrade Tex Geddes as sounding board wrote the first three chapters of what was to become his first published book. Tex was to write: '[Gavin] complained that he was broke, so I told him I was broke too, but his broke and my broke were two entirely different things.' Maxwell returned to London, signed a publishing contract with Rupert Hart-Davis, and over the next year and a half worked at his book. The result of his labours, *Harpoon at a Venture*, was published in 1952 and the first print run quickly sold out. Like many of his subsequent books, *Harpoon at a Venture* was also published in the United States. It is still in print today. The critics applauded the book, the reviewer of *The Times* proclaiming Maxwell to be 'a man of action who writes like a poet'. Applause is all very well, but it doesn't always bring with it money, and *Harpoon at a Venture* wasn't about to restore Maxwell's spent fortune.

In the autumn of 1952, Maxwell borrowed a Land Rover from Monreith and drove down to Sicily in search of material for a second book. He found his subject in the story of Salvatore Giuliano, a Robin Hood figure who had fought for a separatist Sicilian state during the 1940s and been murdered in mysterious circumstances by persons unknown. Maxwell returned to Britain, got himself a literary agent (Graham Watson of Curtis Brown), a new publisher (Longmans), and spent much of the next two years moving between Sicily and London researching the life of Giuliano and working on the manuscript of *God Protect Me from My Friends*. (Maxwell was to return to Sicily in 1955 to work on a second book about the island, *The Ten Pains of Death* – an account of the lives of the Sicilian poor.)

In January 1956, Maxwell accompanied the great wilderness explorer, Wilfred Thesiger, to the marshes of Southern Iraq. He spent two months travelling in that watery wilderness between the Euphrates and Tigris rivers, crumpled up cross-legged in a canoe with Thesiger, and it was there that he was given a five-month-old otter, Mijbil. Maxwell returned to his studio flat in London with the otter and notes enough to produce his next book, *A Reed Shaken by the Wind*, which Thesiger judged 'a brilliant piece of verbal photography'. And I think with *A Reed Shaken by the Wind*, Gavin Maxwell hit his stride.

A small flat in a big city is no place for an otter, and as Mij matured he became more unwieldy and strong. He also had a habit of biting visitors to Maxwell's flat. Maxwell took Mij up to Sandaig with him for the summer and asked Raine to look after Mij there for a time while he went abroad again.

Maxwell returned from abroad and was angry (or perhaps embarrassed – for he had arrived with a friend) to find Raine hadn't vacated the house before his arrival. They had arranged that prior to his return she would spend that night with the family who lived at Tormor, the house up the hill beside the Glenelg road. Maxwell and Raine quarrelled again. In Raine's retelling of the incident in *The Lion's Mouth*, she was being rejected by the man she was in love with and became overwrought. She went out into a gale to climb the rough path to Tormor and the hurt ran so deep that she laid her hands on the trunk of the rowan tree and cried, 'Let Gavin suffer, in this place, as I am suffering now.'

The details of that night, and the phrasing of the curse, differ slightly in the telling. Maxwell's version in *Raven Seek Thy Brother* is a little more sensational. Raine's has to be the truer of the two. Or does it?

Just as I don't believe in ghosts, I'm not so sure I believe in curses. And perhaps neither did Raine, or Maxwell. We all do and say things in hot anger which, with hindsight, we regret, and don't anyway necessarily mean. Raine forever regretted the curse. Whether she believed in her power to blight a life, I cannot say. She was at the time a practising Catholic, intrigued by dreams and their interpretation, by visions, by spiritualism and mysticism. She was a student of the mystic poet and visionary William Blake, and she herself was a poet, with a poet's sensibility and all that goes with that calling.

Looking over their story as I do, from on high and with hindsight and misted facts, Maxwell's flight towards the sun was not far off reaching its zenith anyway. And like Icarus, after melting one's wings off, all that is left is a naturally swift plummet to the sea. Maxwell was careless in many ways – careless of his health, of his businesses, in his treatment of others. And he was a troubled man. Kathleen's curse – when some years later he found out about it – gave him someone (and something suitably exotic) to blame for all the calamities that befell him afterwards.

Raine and Maxwell patched up their differences and continued their uneasy friendship, fighting and forgiving – an abusive marriage of the psyche. Raine continued to look after Mij during Maxwell's periods away. But Mij's demand for constant attendance and attention, without which his energies would turn to the destruction of his surroundings, called for a full-time otter keeper, and to this end Maxwell put out feelers.

In April 1957 Raine travelled to Sandaig with Mij. Mij wandered and was killed by the Glenelg villager Maxwell subsequently wrote of as 'Big Angus'. Whether Mij was killed because all otters were considered vermin back then, or whether the *Lutrogale perspicillata maxwelli* – 'Maxwell's Otter' – was killed due to a local man's antipathy towards its owner, remains moot to this day. Kathleen Raine told Douglas Botting, Maxwell's biographer:

> Mij would have gone eventually, given his propensity for straying, but it was I who was the instrument for evil in Gavin's life. Yet I had meant so intensely to be only the instrument for good. This is something that bewildered and embittered me for many years.

Wilfred Thesiger had other concerns, which he later expressed to Botting:

> [Gavin] had no hand in getting [Mij] and frankly I found it rather odd when he named [the species] after himself – if it was going to be named after anybody it should have been named after me. Gavin owed everything to his trip with me in the marshes. The marshes gave him the otter, the otter gave him *Ring of Bright Water*, and without that he would never have been heard of again.

After Mij's death, Maxwell took over the lease of Raine's Paultons Square house in Chelsea and kept a series of exotic pets: a ring-tailed lemur, a bush baby, a mynah bird, a flock of tanagers . . . but none had the charm or character of Mij, and none of them stayed for long. Raine continued to rent a top-floor flat in the house, but most of her time now was spent in Cambridge, where she had taken up a research fellowship at Girton College to work on a book about William Blake. She eventually moved (some might say she was pushed) out of the house altogether.

In 1957 Maxwell sacked his literary agent. Graham Watson, it seems, had an unfortunate habit of pointing out obstacles and hindrances when Maxwell suggested book ideas and money-making schemes. The possible sale of a film treatment of *Harpoon at a Venture* Maxwell had written hadn't been pursued with much vigour. Maxwell decided that Watson wasn't making enough money for him from his books. Watson, for his part, in *Book Society*, found Maxwell

> a somewhat demanding author. He needed money in substantial amounts and he didn't much mind from whence it came . . . The telephone would ring . . . 'Gavin here. I'm in a garage near Inverness. My super-charger has blown. It's going to cost £150 to repair. I need the cash before my cheque bounces. See if Mark [Longman – Maxwell's publisher] will provide. I'm coming down by sleeper and we'll meet for lunch tomorrow.' I would duly report at the luncheon ren-dezvous to find the impoverished Gavin driving up in a Daimler, temporarily hired to replace his Alvis. Life with Gavin was life on a roller-coaster.

Meanwhile Maxwell had met Peter Janson-Smith, an employee of Watson's literary agency who was setting up on his own as an agent and who had a positive, can-do approach to business. Janson-Smith became Maxwell's literary agent and it was he, together with Maxwell's publisher and editor, who encouraged Maxwell to write *Ring of Bright Water*.

By 1959, Maxwell had written four books and was fed up. His work had been praised in the press (*Harpoon at a Venture* had been the *Daily Mail* Book of the Month, *A Reed Shaken by the Wind* had won the Heinemann Award of the Royal Society of Literature, and almost all had carried Book Society recommendations) but it hadn't brought him the wealth he'd hoped for. And as you may have surmised by now, Maxwell was a spendthrift – however much money he had, it was never enough. Lack of money slowed him down and thwarted his dreams, and he resented it, he who'd been born to it.

A book about Sandaig and the pet otter that had brought his West Highland home and himself so alive seemed to all concerned to be just the thing, and in the spring of 1959 Maxwell withdrew to Sandaig to write it. He took with him Jimmy Watt – a school-leaver he had recently employed. Jimmy, Maxwell had determined, would look after Sandaig during Maxwell's absences, and a Scottish otter cub that he would take from the wild once they arrived.

Fate intervened.

Not long after settling in at Sandaig, sitting over a whisky in the Lochalsh Hotel in Kyle with Raef Payne, who'd journeyed north for a holiday, Maxwell spied a man and a woman by the Skye ferry slipway taking an otter for a walk. He rushed out of the hotel, accosted the couple with stories of Mij and his search for a replacement otter, and a few weeks later Edal (a female, a future starlet) took up residence at Sandaig.

Ring of Bright Water, published the following year, brought Maxwell what he desired – a global readership and an embarrassment of riches. And he deserved it. He was good, believe me; one of the best. And he was *funny*, and clever.*

When you don't have much money (and Maxwell, for all his flash, after the failure of Soay Shark Fisheries had little), life is simple because you have few options and therefore very little choice. Money in large amounts brings with it (besides substantial tax demands) opportunities. It brings temptation and freedoms undreamt of, but it can't by itself bring contentment, nor can it, as the song goes, buy love. Success makes life complicated. And Maxwell's life was complicated enough as it was.

When Maxwell sat down to write the book which was to make his name, did he knowingly create a mythical version of himself: 'Gavin Maxwell, reclusive otter man'?

---

* Here I *should* give you a précis of *Ring of Bright Water*, and later on I *should* provide you with workmanlike précis of Maxwell's other books. But I don't want to. If you're interested, find the books and read them. Read them all.

I don't believe he did. It looks to me like he wrote the truth, more or less, as remembered. The manuscript of *Ring of Bright Water* – Maxwell's sepia-ink calligraphy fills several battered blue notebooks – is too fluently written to be artful. There are very few emendations or rewritten passages. Much of it was written sitting by the waterfall at Sandaig, and there is much joy in that book. The myth, I think, was placed upon him by his readers and the media, another case of typecasting. If we can pigeonhole someone, put him in a cage and label him, we think we've got a handle on him. We know what he is and what it is he deals in. But our moods change continually. We've daytime and night-time selves, idle times and feeling-sorry-for-ourselves times, bouts of achievement and bouts of lying on the sofa gazing passively into the goggle-box. We've sexually efflorescent times and periods when our romantic life is as barren as a megabarchan sand dune marching across the emptiest quarter of the Empty Quarter. We've good days and bad. We are all many selves. If we live long we pass through at least three generations and our morals and casuistries, our consciousness and our interests, our tastes and our motivations will change often during our journeying. How to judge?

≈

The stack of Sunday newspapers by the door of my room grew taller. Sandy informed me of the Five Winter Rule:

'If you can stick that many up here, you'll become a local. You never know, you might even stay forever.'

A warm ocean current, the North Atlantic Drift, flows up the west coast of Britain and keeps the western sea a few degrees above that of the east. West-coast weather is wet and windy; east-coast weather drier but colder. On the island frost was rare. All through December and January there was snow on the mountaintops, like a sprinkling of sugar, but none on the island or in the two villages. Driving to Inverness one January morning I came to a line stretching right across the land, clearly dividing it in two. To the west – the island, Hebridean, side – rain fell on moorland and bare mountainside; and to the east – snow. I stopped the car to wonder, then drove under a rainbow onto a road carpeted in white.

The constantly changing weather is an integral part of life up there. You are always aware of it. A benign and picturesque morning might be followed by a depressingly dreich week. The salt-laden sea air rusts metal zips in jackets and trousers. Everything rusts, or turns green – even if it isn't made of metal, even if it isn't left out in the rain. Sometimes it felt as if we were merely subjects ruled by the monarchical weather, which rolled regally on and by, capricious, bipolar, and emotionally draining. Like the little girl in the children's book – when the Highlands are good, they are very, very good; but when they are bad they are horrid. And though we followed the weather – watched the reports on the TV and tuned into radio bulletins; and though we dressed in expectation of rain – sea-booted and water-proofed denizens everywhere – we rarely discussed it. In good company, 'bad' weather becomes an irrelevance.

I'd been on the island some months before it struck me that I never saw anyone carrying an umbrella. It seemed odd in a place with so much rain. I bought one and the first chance I got (the very next day) I opened it out and held it aloft on a walk to the shops. Before I'd reached the end of the bridge a wind came blasting down the loch at forty miles an hour and blew my sweat-shop manufactured umbrella inside out. I flapped about by the side of the road for a short while, flailing around in the wind and driving rain, but I understood. The same goes for broad-brimmed hats.

To begin with I worked around the weather, but soon learnt that you have to just keep going. Council workmen carry on strimming the verges through rainstorms, diggers and tractors still roll, roofers and builders carry on hammering, fishermen stay out among flinging, foaming waves. And it can be exhilarating out there in Weather – wild and raw; energising and enervating all at the same time. I said as much to Sandy one day.

'Makes *you* feel alive, maybe,' he said. 'Not much fun being out there in a blizzard though, or setting off to Kyle in fine weather and having to plough back to Kyleakin through icy-cold horizontal rain, raindrops sharp as needles flying into your eyes.'

I remember battling my way up one of the Cuillins in a rainstorm and the rain and the wind so loud, knocking me around, finding ways to douse me between the fibres of my 'waterproof' clothing; a pair of ravens rising in the air like kites to play and sail higher into the heavens. I bellowed into the tempest and it bellowed back, far louder, far madder, its voice higher and bleaker than my own. I remember standing under the Skye Bridge watching squalls come blasting down from the Minch in the north, the wind screaming, buffeting solid objects and rushing swishing through the grass and reeds and the dying bracken and fireweed. West Highland wind stops you in your tracks. The wind frequently forces the closure of the Skye Bridge to lorries and vans. The wind shunts parked cars (one of them mine!) several feet to the right. The wind blows cold and warm and fierce, and screams. The wind is without morals or scruples, qualms or remorse. People die up there every year. Climbers get caught out and get blown off a hill or down a ravine. In January 2005 a hurricane ripped through the Hebrides, wrecking and flattening and tearing to tatters. Fish-farm floats five-foot square were torn from their moorings, boats were blown out to sea and caravans flipped upside down. On South Uist in the Outer Hebrides, a 125 mph wind killed three generations of one family when the car in which they were travelling was blown off the road and into the sea. Every village still misses a son, a father, a grandfather who headed out to sea and never came back. Death, up there, is only a wrong foot away.

Rain would fall for days without pause before I'd awaken one morning aware that something had changed: the banging on the Velux had stopped, the wind had blown itself out; it was over. The sun had come and the world outside glistened. Voices travelled across from Kyleakin. Kids rode their bikes, kicked a football about the green, played shinty and loitered about on the beach, sneaking cigarettes. Grown-ups littered benches outside the pubs, elderly tourists sipped tea on collapsible chairs in the car park. I'd cast off in my dinghy to clear my head of the fug, out on clear waters beneath a blazing sun, puttering above fat-fingered starfish, porcupine-needled sea urchins and bone-coloured barnacles. Over there by the skerries, the flap-flap-glide of a shearwater; and here come the kitti-wakes, out of an empty blue sky. They hover overhead, follow the boat for a while, look down at me, look up and wheel away towards the Crowlin Isles. I cut the engine. Apart from the rumble of a waterfall and the bubbling call of a curlew, there is nothing. Utter silence and nobody. It is strong medicine. Night falls and a cobweb of stars hangs overhead, where for days there has been only murk and rags of dishwater cloud.

≈

I received a steady trickle of polite, bland letters from literary agents informing me that my *Travels* book wasn't something they felt they could sell to a publisher (*any publisher, anywhere in the known universe?*) just now, that the market was flat just now, that they weren't taking on new clients just now, that they wished me good luck with my writing, with future projects I might be foolish enough to embark on, etcetera, etcetera, etc. Literary taste is subjective, I said to myself. Ask six friends to read the same book and they'll give you six differing opinions of it. Ever fallen in love with a book and wanted your best friends to love it too, only to find that they hate it? What's treasure to one man is to another just junk that should have been chucked in the bin years ago. (Why does Sandy come to mind when I write that?)

But I knew I'd failed with *Travels*, knew that it wasn't good enough. And that, more importantly, *I* wasn't good enough. Before coming to the island I had churned out seven guidebooks in four years and I never wanted to research another. Writing guidebooks isn't all it's cracked up to be. What I wanted to write wasn't going anywhere, and writing was *tough*. I was constantly assailed by self-doubt, self-loathing, and a realization of the triviality of my 'calling'. No one – not even family and friends – thought it was a sensible occupation, or any kind of occupation at all. 'Still scribbling?' they'd ask. 'Had a best-seller yet? Sold the film rights? Aha-ha-ha.' I was fed up with those 'poor, mad fool' looks of sympathy I got whenever I was stupid enough to let slip I was 'working on a book'. And even when my guidebooks had been published the money I earned from all that work had been rubbish. I put the typescript of *Travels* and my hopes away, and in my mind I crossed out in thick black marker the idea of 'Author' as a career option. I'd have to think up another way to earn a living.

≈

I hadn't seen any robins for weeks when one flew into the bothy, fluttered around in circles, crashed into a window and dropped in a heap on my desk. It picked itself up, took off, missed the open doorway and bonked into the window again. This happened three times. I raised my arm gently, pointed to the door and quietly told the robin to stop being brainless and make for that. The robin flew into the window again, then flew to the space heater, dropped to the flagstone floor and chirped a pathetic chirrup. I bent down to it and it stepped onto my outstretched finger. I took it outside. It sat on my finger for a moment, chirruped loudly at me, exerted a feather-light pressure on my hand, and flew away.

By mid-February the trees on the island were in bud and the paths, after rain, crawled with slugs, some of which ate each other. By the end of the month daffodils, the descendants of those planted as bulbs decades ago by the lighthouse keepers, were pushing through the same spot where Richard Frere had mentioned them growing in the spring of 1965: 'a mass of unexpected daffodils brightened the slope below the cottage.'

Robins flew at each other, bickered endlessly and chased the chaffinches. One morning I watched a pine marten sneaking along. I stood stock-still behind the half-windowed door of my room. We were only seven feet apart, the pine marten and I, and it knew something wasn't quite right. It froze, stretched its tail out behind it, stalked round the corner and was gone. It was the only one I ever saw on the island.

I watched a shrew attempting to get at peanuts in a feeder I'd hung from a short length of broom handle stuck in the front lawn. The shrew inched up the broom handle like a caterpillar, lost its grip and toppled into the grass. It did this again and again. I felt like Robert the Bruce watching his spider, and the message was almost the same – 'If at first you don't succeed, try, try and try again', but my shrew was a complete failure and I began to feel sorry for it. I fetched bread, squatted low and shuffled along the lawn, throwing chunks of bread towards the hungry shrew as I went. The shrew twitched its pointy, whiskered nose but didn't eat. I held out a piece. The shrew sniffed, elongated its little body and sank long nicotine-coloured rodent teeth into the fleshy pad of my middle finger. I squealed. I shook my hand. The shrew, its body flying from side to side, hung on grimly. I shook my hand more fiercely and the shrew spun off it into long grass. Bright blood dripped from my finger. The shrew emerged from the long grass, looked about myopically, sniffed, and catching my scent sniffed some more and advanced. I retreated, reminded of the story of a fur trapper found dead in his Alaskan log cabin long ago. The trapper's skeleton, collapsed in an armchair, had been picked clean and the man who found it had opened the cabin door to be faced with a sniffing, murderous, moving carpet of shrews.

Towards the end of February, while I was driving to the start of a cliff-top ramble on Skye with a full load of trustees squashed into my car, something under the bonnet went *clunk!* I pumped the accelerator but got no response. I steered for the side of the road and we rolled silently to a halt beside a loch. Below us a gull was flapping its wings in a fury, struggling with something or other as usual; a lone dabchick paddled unconcernedly by. I opened the bonnet of my car. The trustees and I peered in and jiggled a lead or two and I tried the ignition. Nothing. The heaviest of my passengers (and somewhere not so very deep inside myself I was already blaming his weight for overtaxing my car) telephoned to Kyle for a taxi. I telephoned a garage. The damage turned out to be serious, and costly. The lemon had run out of juice. I scrapped it. From now on I could walk to the shops, or take the dinghy.

My world shrank considerably, my life confined to the few square miles of sea and rock surrounding me. But I didn't mind. The creatures on the island kept me company. And the people in the cities and clogged urban spaces were doing what they always did whenever I looked. And there was always Ewan the stalker's train at the station in Kyle waiting to take me back to them if I needed.

Hi-Arts, the Highland arts organization I'd asked to look at my work-in-progress, sent me an email. The assessor had been impressed and the organization was offering me a complimentary place on a week-long residential writers' 'masterclass' at a retreat on the north-east coast of Scotland at the end of April. A literary agent would be attending and wanted to meet me.

L-shaped. We have to keep going, keep pressing on.

≈

We'd been sitting over a few too many pints by the fire in the pub in Isleornsay. It was a filthy day outside but the atmosphere in the pub was as convivial and lubricated as you can get.

Sandy placed his pint glass soundlessly on the table.

'Since the end of the seventies, coinciding with Thatcher's Conservative government and its policies, Britain has changed almost beyond recognition. Not for the better, neither. We're all richer, sure, but poverty's relative. Even the poorest estate-dwelling, dole-drawing no-hoper's got more than he knows what to do with. He'll have his wide-screen satellite TV, stereo system and mobile phone. He'll run a car. He's got more than me! He's not poor. Let him go to Afghanistan or Africa if he wants to understand just how not-poor he is. All these scroungers, whining on about how "unfair" it all is, how badly off they are, they haven't an effing clue.'

I stared into the fire. When Sandy was on a roll there was nothing you could do to stop him.

'And we're not allowed to be amateurs any more. We've all got to be "professionals" now. "Experts". Those poor people, told to work hard and get that promotion, climb the career ladder and get on, "You'll be well rewarded!" And there're all these non-jobs they've got nowadays: management consultancy. I ask you! Did you know a window cleaner's not called a window cleaner any more, oh no!, he's a "vision-clearance executive". I stacked shelves in Co-op once. D'you know what it said on my pay-slip? "Job Title: Ambient Replenishment Operative". A paper shuffler is now an "officer"; middle-managers are "executive officers" and managers "chief executive officers". What a joke! I tell you, next time you get to a city just you sit down at a train station during morning rush hour and watch all those poor ants scurrying to work, yawning, pasty-faced, tired, worried. And they're all off to do what? What is the point of those jobs they're all rushing off to do? Those poor, poor people. Office fodder, that's what they are.

Living in a world of blah, living on credit, and working their guts out to keep paying off the debt they've sunk into just so's they can keep up with the Joneses.

'I get in one of those fascist modern cars and it won't let me drive anywhere until I've put my seatbelt on, and the engine's so complicated it needs a computer to tell a mechanic what's wrong! And CCTV everywhere and rules about this and that and being cautioned all the time to "take care" and "watch out" and nannied in train stations and airports by anonymous patronizing suety-voiced announcers; over-regulated, over-governed . . . It's like *1985!*'

'You mean *1984*,' I said. 'It's a good book that. Orwell was an interesting man. One of the things he said was: "At fifty, everyone has the face he deserves." There's another goo—'

'And we watch the news on TV, hear the reports on the radio, read the misery in the newspapers and all the time we're bombarded with versions of the same message, "It's a terrible, big bad world out there so stay in your home! Keep your children indoors! Murder, rape and terrorism! It's everywhere! You're surrounded! Out-of-control drug-crazed teenagers and another pensioner got her head bashed in yesterday for the measly eight pounds twenty pence she had in her purse." Aagh!'

Sandy drew breath, took a sip of his pint. I took my eyes from the fire and looked around. At a nearby table a pretty

young woman in a red velvet dress was whispering loudly
to a friend, '. . . and there he was, washing his *balls* in the
sink!'

'Twenty-first century England and most of "Great" –
ha! – Britain,' Sandy went on, 'is isolating and boring.
The villages are empty – they're dead! Oldsters indoors
watching daytime TV and the young away working in
air-conditioned offices in town. And in the evenings they're
still dead, the villages, everyone stuck inside watching
moronic TV shows that are turning them into dummies.
So *unnatural* we've become. The farms have been sold off
to "heritage" quangos and the farmers who still farm are
paid not to grow anything. A lot of the countryside is dead
too. Look at the Lake District – pretty, but dead. Land
isn't worked any more, it's "husbanded". And every year
more of it gets carved up and sold off for yet another
road-building scheme.

'I hate the way Britain has changed. The sugar-and-fat-
and-salt-laden fast food that we're offered and the growing
obesity of everyone and the aggressive driving and all this
shopping – this *consuming* – everyone *has* to do. Messed-up
schooling producing dense chav kids with no common-
sense, who turn into whining adults who possess even less
sense of social responsibility than they did when they were
kids. Teenage girls who get pregnant so they can get a
council house and benefits and feed fast food to their kids
because they don't know how or can't be bothered to cook,

and so then their kids never learn how to, or care. And on it goes.

'And the high streets dying and all looking the same with the supermarkets and chain stores vacuuming up everyone's money while the independent shops unable to compete close down. And all this choice we're offered of things to buy, but almost all of it pap. Britain's not great anymore, Dan, it's bankrupt. What do we produce now? Tell me. What? Everything is imported. It makes me sad. It really does.'

Sandy broke off to waggle his empty glass at me.

I got a round in.

'Thanks. But all that, all that . . . *garbage*, is a long way from up here, thank God. The local teenagers hang out by the bus stop in Kyle, but there's never the sense of threat like you'd feel down south. This place works. We more or less police ourselves. People leave you alone, give you your space, but will help if you ask them to. Most of the work people do up here has a point to it at least. And yes, I know there's gossip – there always is in small communities – but you have the space to get away from it, from everyone. And there's that sense of adventure and danger out at sea or on the hill – that sense of mortality . . . it humbles us all.'

We drank on until our money ran out. There wasn't an ATM within twenty miles. We walked out into a gale to hitch a lift back to Kyleakin.

'God, the weather up here gets me down sometimes,'

Sandy called, over the blow. 'I start cracking on with converting *Ebb 'n Flow* and then it blows a hooley and I have to down tools again. Sometimes I wonder if she'll ever be finished.'

We walked on down the road. No cars were passing. We weaved our way on through the black night.

≈

Johnny Ach telephoned. He'd been to see Jimmy Watt. They'd hatched a plan to revive the fortunes of Kyleakin and the Kyleakin Lighthouse Island Trust. Jimmy Watt knew of a decommissioned lightship up for sale somewhere in England. The lightship would be acquired, brought north and moored in Kyleakin Marina. Money would be raised and the lightship restored. A new national museum concentrating on lightships, lighthouses and lighthouse keepers would be established right here in tiny Kyleakin. The entrance money would be shared between the Kyleakin Lighthouse Island Trust and other deserving causes in Kyleakin and Kyle. It was practically a done deal, Johnny Ach told me. He had all the right contacts.

Then he went and died.

Five

Quicksands, Scottish History and a Thrupenny Bit

I got a lift to the Catholic church with one of the trustees. We walked down from the car park to merge with a sea of mourners standing in the sharp frosty air outside the church. I stood behind a naval officer, smart in his black serge uniform, and spotted many of the trustees in the crowd, and Susan Browning, and Pete, and Ewan, John the chairman and Marcus, the Kyle lifeboat crew in their kit, Sandy . . . There were other faces I'd seen in the villages, and many I hadn't. A white-haired man I thought might be Jimmy Watt stood a few feet away. The silent shuffling congregation stretched from the doors of the church to the shores of Loch Long. A loudspeaker had been set up on a bench so we could all hear the stentorian tones of the priest expounding his views on death and the afterlife. Celebration of a full and useful life was sidelined in favour of a hectoring lecture on the more important matter of earning one's place beside God in heaven. After a long time the priest stopped squawking and a hymn was sung and prayers said. I turned my gaze to the godless crows and jackdaws flying free above the churchyard. Up on the surrounding hills the backsliding sheep – so far away they looked like puffballs – grazed unconcernedly. The freezing fog of four hundred exhalations coalesced above us. The priest's haverings warmed the air again before silence, the shuffling of boots on gravel, a cough, a sob.

Johnny Ach's coffin was wheeled from the church on a trolley. The builder from Kyle, his face as dangerously florid as Johnny's had been in life, stood beside the church-yard gate and called out how it was going to be. In the Highlands, by tradition, the builder is also the undertaker. Johnny had been a big man, in many ways, and a heavy one. There would be a changeover of bearers to carry the coffin to the hearse, which would transport the departed to the Clan Macrae cemetery at the head of the loch. The cortège began, Johnny's family followed, a flood streamed slowly behind them, a slipstream of grievers, rememberers, well-wishers.

We stood by drooping snowdrops on a hillside above Clachanduich cemetery; a piper on a hillock played a lament. Men wearing the team colours of Johnny's shinty club lined the path to the grave. The immortal mountains surrounded us. We stood to the keening of pipes, the swishing of the wind through the heather, the gargle of a brook on its way to the sea. It wasn't alcohol in the end. It was his heart that, aged fifty, did for Johnny. I don't even know if Johnny drank.

≈

Before I went to live in the Highlands I had always viewed small communities with a great deal of suspicion. I'd seen them as quicksand – pretty deadly – and whenever I'd found myself near one I trod very carefully so as to remain free from its strictures. I was always watching my step, and had always done so. It was what my 'non-book' *Travels* had been about – the avoidance of getting 'bogged down'. But over that spring on the island something strange, and happy, began to happen to me. Villagers, strangers I'd seen in the shops and had passed along the roads of Kyle or Kyleakin, raised an arm in salutation and smiled or nodded and said hello when our paths crossed. With time I gained confidence and would stop to chat and take in the day with them. When one evening I walked into the bar of the Lochalsh Hotel and the barmaid smiled and said, 'Will it be the usual?' I felt I'd been accepted at last, sort of. Finding your way in a small community isn't about getting sucked down to death by a treacherous patch of quicksand, it's about finding soil fertile enough in which to take root. I hadn't understood this before. It takes time to find where you fit, but we all find our place in the end.

~

I have come to the conclusion that there are five levels to a Highland community:

1. NATIVES

Natives 'belong' in the Highlands. Their ties to the land go back generations. They went to school in the Highlands and have a wide circle of friends, family and business connections locally. They tend to live in modern housing and council houses, work for the Highland Council (the only provider of for-life jobs up here) or the utility companies (telephone, electricity, water, etc.). Natives may have left the Highlands at some point in their lives – for work, for love, to travel – and have returned to settle, raise a family and grow old amongst friends and relatives.

Natives tend to socialize within their own stratum and don't have much time for anyone below the level of Local (*see below*) because these others are often transient and any links forged will be broken soon enough. What's the point of making a friend of someone who'll shortly be away out the door? Many Natives have ancestral links to pioneering East Coast fishing folk, Lowland Scots and Glaswegians who moved to the Highlands during the boom times of many years ago and stayed on.

With such strong ties to the area, Natives may own crofting land which, once it has been 'de-crofted', can be sold for £70,000 and more per third of an acre plot. For many a Native, brought up in a land where life is hard and money scarce, a bird in the hand is well worth selling to the nearest cat and it doesn't matter much where that cat or its money comes from. Unfortunately, selling off parcels of crofting land as building plots to Incomers (*see below*) has led to many a dispute over land use and rights of access.

Natives are the most grounded of the inhabitants of the Highlands, the most 'normal' of all. There are, for instance, very few Native 'artists'. Natives belong.

2. LOCALS

Locals have lived in the area for 'many years' – sometimes as few as five, perhaps as many as twenty. (After that, a Local, if well integrated, could almost but not quite be classed as a Native.) Locals may be retired, or young couples with children attending local schools, or childless refugees or misfits from the South. Locals will sometimes affect a Highland accent to show that they have been living in the area 'for ages'. Retired Locals with a pension do not necessarily need to find employment but, with all that free time, have to *do* something and so occasionally attend the winter talks. They will sit on all sorts of committees and community councils if they can find a way in.

Because they have lived in the area for quite some time, most Locals will have got their Highland life in order – gardens planned and laid out, some kind of income-source and a small circle of, mainly Local, friends. Locals will mix as often as possible with Natives, but are aware of the wide gulf that separates them and those who have lived up here 'forever'. They have accepted that Natives are a different breed and they have come to accept their parvenu status in the community.

The more useful Locals (i.e. those who have a trade, rather than paint stones and call themselves Artists) are sought-after members of the community. A skilled trades-man will have more work than he can handle, take on too much (after all, you can't afford to turn down a job when you're self-employed), and end up juggling customers and letting many of them down. Distances between jobs are vast. The round trip between Kyle and Inverness, for example, is about 170 miles. Tradesmen are always in demand in the Highlands. Even the most slapdash, unprin-cipled and disorganized plumber, electrician, plasterer or joiner will be welcomed with smiles and open arms when he eventually turns up to get on with the job he originally promised to have finished by twelve weeks last Wednesday at the very latest.

Locals ploughed their way through their first five win-ters up here years ago and the Highlands have become home.

3. INCOMERS, WHITE SETTLERS, BLOW-INS

These three, interchangeable, terms all refer to that rather lonesome and forlorn creature – the recent immigrant. If he (or, of course, she) can find a viable way to make a living, can hack the winters, tread softly and not irritate the neighbours, he may, once he has done his time, become a Local – although unless he is young, never a Native. (Incomers of Lowland Scots extraction, however, being of the blood, will often fast-track to Local status.)

Incomers are often English and many come from urban areas. A Welsh or Irish Incomer, or a Continental, is as rare a sight as a hoopoe in the Highlands, although there is a smattering of North American and Canadian Incomers who have 'come home' to the land of their emigrant forefathers. A disproportionate number of Incomers are middle-aged, unmarried and childless. (I can offer the reader no analysis of this; it remains a mystery to me.) There are also a large number of retired Incomers who have accumulated the wealth to acquire their dream – a pretty property in a superlative location. Here they can live out the years that remain to them, eking out their superannuation payments and/or disability allowance, create a garden and study the flora and fauna around them. Because of the small population of the Highlands, healthcare up here is enviable – hospital waiting lists are short and the elderly and infirm receive a superior service. This reason alone has spurred many an Incomer to head for the Highlands.

A small number of Incomers are dreamers, but these characters rarely last long and are more Tourist (*see below*) than Incomer. Incomers include: refugees from 'normal' life who move to the Highlands to escape a society down south that moves too fast for them, assorted eccentrics and adventurers, and the wonderful, hardworking Eastern Europeans – who have taken the building and hospitality trades by storm.

Incomers are (overly) keen to 'get involved' with local community projects and are often stunned to find themselves shunned or marginalized by the Natives and Locals (who know what wanting to 'get involved' really means). Highland Council jobs are not generally available to Incomers, who tend to figure large in the voluntary sector. Some Incomers move to the Highlands with the idea of establishing a business, but all too often the business proves to be unviable, finances become overstretched and panic and misery ensue. Many Incomers take to gardening and staring out at the rain from their caravan windows. The younger members of this substratum, appreciating the proximity of mountains and sea, take up climbing, sailing and kayaking (activities that Natives, especially, see little point in). Older Incomers attend the talks, lectures and rambles, much as the Locals used to, before they lost interest.

Incomers are known to announce their imminent arrival by placing an advertisement under the 'Accommodation Wanted' section of the local newspaper. An example I have taken from a copy of an April 2006 *West Highland Free Press* reads:

Married couple, he a carpenter/aspiring photographer; she a housewife/aspiring writer, wanting to settle in and raise a family in the North West Highlands, Lewis or Harris. Seek secluded cottage/house/static caravan in rural area.

The names of the couple follow, together with an email address and a phone number – the code of which denotes a location in the south of England.

Incomers are really only one step up from,

4. Tourists

Tourists flood the Highlands between late June and early September, but a steady trickle runs through the region at all times of the year now, with spikes at Easter, Christmas and New Year. Tourism is important to the Highlands and a vital source of income for all strata mentioned above. The tourist season brings with it the reopening of hostelries and catering businesses after the long winter recess, and the staging of events such as ceilidhs and folk music 'sessions' in pubs and community centres, which are appreciated by all.

Tourists in camper vans are a cause of a certain amount of ire and grumbling from Highlanders, mainly because the supremely self-sufficient camper vanners don't bring much to the party. Those with camper vans stock up at supermarkets in Glasgow and Fort William on the way north, and litter the bays and machair with their vehicles and barbecues. Their main spend is with the ferry company, Caledonian MacBrayne, petrol stations and, occasionally, pub landlords.

Caravanners are viewed with even more suspicion and ire (clogging up roads, slowing everyone down), but due to the hilly nature of the terrain these are fewer in number.

It is good to see the Tourists arriving after a long winter and equally it is good to see them go away again in the autumn.

5. SECOND HOME OWNERS

Second Home Owners and Holiday Cottage Owners seldom intrude on a Highland community as most aren't seen from one year to the next. A Second Home Owner visits his postcard-pretty possession infrequently and never for long. (Gavin Maxwell, for the first fifteen years or so of his tenancy of Sandaig, belonged to this stratum. Before the arrival of the otters, he used the house as a retreat, never a home.)

There appears to exist a division between those who have owned a holiday cottage for a generation or two (who are considered and consider themselves a cut above the rest) and those who have bought more recently. As available properties have become scarcer and prices have increased, the Natives have come to resent these wealthy materialists, who buy and renovate yet hardly ever use.

Incomers, usually from areas of higher earning potential (i.e. southern England), have also pushed up house prices and are similarly condemned. Equally galling for the Natives and the Locals (and the poor benighted Incomers), many second homes are bought as an investment and business opportunity. A well-appointed holiday cottage in a picturesque setting can be let in the high season to Tourists for up to and sometimes over £1,000 per week. (A third of the houses in the pretty village of Plockton – down the road from Kyle and the setting of the BBC's *Hamish Macbeth* television series – are holiday homes.)

Second Home Owners and the high prices paid for houses by rich Incomers prevent young Natives and the children of Locals from buying a house in the neighbourhood in which they were raised. This is one of the reasons why the majority of Natives and young Locals live in new-builds and council housing. Another factor, though, is that Highlanders are of a more practical mind than most Incomers and Second Home Owners – new-builds tend to be better insulated and less cramped than traditional stone white houses, renovation is expensive and, as I have already pointed out, reliable tradesmen are as scarce as hen's teeth.

≈

In March, after a week of dry Siberian wind, I awoke to a stillness that could mean only one thing. We seem to know when it happens. I went to the door of my room and pulled the thick curtain aside.

Snow, great flakes of it, falling, covering the island in a smooth white blanket. It hushed. I got dressed and went out into it.

Otter tracks. I followed them along the cobbled path. They came to an abrupt end. I searched about me. There on the top of the wall. The otter had leapt up, run along the top of it and bounded back down onto the path. More tracks led from the slipway to the doors of the cottage before doubling back to the slip, where my dinghy lay half-hidden by snow. The otter had been in the dinghy, rolled around in it – really squirmed – then back out onto the slipway and into the bay. There were bird prints too: a hopped circle, a line leading to a larger hopped circle, another line, another circle; eccentric, dizzying motifs; like an absentminded professor, eyes to the ground, lost in thought, twirling around in the street, bird-brained.

The snow lay thick for a week and then it was gone. And in its place – spring.

Clover and vetch appeared under the bridge, and daisies and buttercups along the cobbled path. Violets blushed and carpets of bluebells covered the slope where on Workcrew Wednesdays John had scythed away brambles and bracken. By the end of March the fragrance of honeysuckle wafted around the bothy. Dunnocks came back to hop among the brambles, and the first curly fronds of bracken unfurled like beckoning fingers in rewind.

In the first week of April I spotted the first 'woolly bear' of the year, and a bumblebee. The redwings returned, filling the night sky with a high-pitched *tssiiii-ssiiii-ssiiii* as flocks flew over the island on their way to Scandinavia. Seals returned to the skerries with their crying, keening pups; Adam-Ant-eyed razorbills returned, squadrons of black guillemots returned to race over the Inner Sound and, further out, puffins chuckled and growled. Greylags, readying themselves to head north to the Arctic, stomped restlessly on the grassy patches above East Bay.

Gulls – common gulls, herring gulls, black-headed gulls, lesser and greater black-backed gulls – took it in turns to stand on the chimney pots to jeer at each other and to cast a beady eye over me as I pottered about below. Lighting the fire in the Long Room one day I heard squawks coming down the chimney. On going outside to see what all the commotion was about I found a herring gull standing on the pot, gabbling and waggling its rump, warming itself like an old gent standing with his back to the fire.

Gulls – for all their beauty of plumage, their Jonathan Livingstone Seagull aeronautical prowess – seem a bad-tempered lot, eternally affronted and peevish. I placed scraps of food on Lookout Point every day and as soon as I'd dropped them gulls would arrive from all directions out of a seemingly empty sky. The first to land would plant a webbed foot on the piece of potato or whatever, stretch out its wings, stick its beak in the air and start screeching. 'Back Off! Get Back! Mine! You! YES, YOU! Get Back! Back, I say! Just get BACK, can't you!' before getting so harried and flustered it would lose command of the situation and find its place taken by another, larger gull, who would be similarly tormented by its greed and its competitors until its position would be usurped by another. And so it would go on. Gulls appear to share none of the communal spirit of, say, chickens, though they live longer. I read of one living to forty-nine.

Along with the grass, the numbers of tourists began to grow. I heard again the grinding of gears of heavily laden camper vans accelerating up and over the bridge above me. The bramble tendrils, like triffids, were on the move again and the bracken and docks were gaining the upper hand. I coped for a while on my own, chopping and pulling, but with spring becoming riotous it was time to call in the Wednesday Workcrew.

We got on with repairs to the lighthouse keepers' cottage. After several memos and meetings, the trustees agreed that the repairing of the gable-end wall was a necessity. A local builder, with an accent so gentle there seemed more Irish in it than Scots, came to price the job. He ran a finger along the brickwork and held it up to show me a lump of gunk on the end of it. 'Old mortar,' he said. 'It's saturated. Most of this wall needs repointing. Take about five days.'

A few weeks later he returned with his mate, carrying ladders, scaffolding, mallets and cold chisels. It was good to hear voices and laughter again. The weather stayed fine. On 20 April I saw the first swallow, and six days later I heard the first cuckoo. Insects dropped into cups of tea with infuriating regularity.

I took my dinghy down the loch to see if I couldn't get her to sail. I couldn't, and nearly drowned. The Seagull, recalcitrant museum piece that it was, refused to start and a strong katabatic wind got up and blew me down towards an abandoned fish farm whose steel pontoons and cages clanged and banged like tolling bells tolling for me. I really thought I was going to die that day.

Pete Baggeley invited me to join his team of Incomers, 'The Skye Terriers', for the fortnightly Kyleakin Quiz Night. Villagers donated prizes – whisky, unwanted birth-day presents, wine, a plaster figurine, beer, a big box of biscuits, a brand new toaster, a carton of duty-free cigar-ettes.

Pete was surprisingly competitive and gave us pep talks, and to start with he believed in us. 'This night,' he'd whis-per as we sat mentally preparing ourselves for the questions, 'is our night. Now come on, team, think! And let's win this one.' Then the chain-smoking quiz-maestro, Malcolm – moonlighting from his day job as local telephone engineer

– would pace back and forth across the community centre, puffing away and hollering out questions.

A team calling itself 'The Friends of King Malcolm' always won by a mile; with other Kyleakin Native teams collecting the rest of the prizes. As Malcolm read out the answers, Pete would put a hand, once again, to his brow and let it slide down his anguished face. The categories of Malcolm's quiz were always the same: Geography, Sport, General Knowledge, Natural History and, most importantly and cunningly, *Scottish* History. We Incomers never stood a chance, which was just how Malcolm and the Natives liked to play it.

With the repointing completed, we painted. The buildings hadn't seen paint in years. Over two weeks of warm dry weather, we bleach-washed and whitewashed the cottage, the bothy and the lighthouse shed.

I got the Seagull working and asked Sandy to come out in the dinghy to teach me to sail.

He sprawled in the bottom of the boat looking on and chuckling quietly as I grappled with the rig. There was barely a breath of wind anyway.

'Give up,' he drawled. 'Give up! The mast's no good. That sail's far too big for the boat. The boom's set too low. The mainsheet you've rigged is all wrong. You'll never get her to go. You've been sold a dud, Dan. Give up!'

I told him I'd bought the boat from an ex-policeman.

'They're the worst!' he said, and hooted all the more.

We weren't out for long.

A few weeks later the Kyle Flotilla races started up again. I abandoned the trustee and his smart yellow sloop and sailed that season with Sandy in *Emma Gaze*, crewing alongside an ever-changing cast of strays that Sandy picked up in the pubs, cafes, and hostels he frequented around the place. Sandy believed a day's sailing to be a balm for all ills and the more people he could introduce to the joys of sailing, the better life would be, though whether for himself or the waifs he coerced onto his boat to crew for him I've still not quite decided.

We never won a prize.

≈

There was a tumbledown, roofless shed on the island that once housed the lighthouse keepers' hens. In Maxwell's day, this henhouse had been converted to accommodate the surviving otter, Teko. I used the shed for storing firewood, which I covered with a plastic sheet to keep off the rain. One day Sandy and I were in the shed rooting around for a board to mix cement on to fill some of the cracks in the paving around the cottage. I was scrabbling around, pulling out old timbers, when I noticed a book-sized lump of concrete with lettering on it.

'Look at this,' I said, passing it to Sandy.

'Just a piece of the old rendering.'

'Yes, but look.'

I took the lump from Sandy and rubbed away moss and dirt. Sandy peered over my shoulder.

'A. S. . . . 19 . . . 68.'

'Andrew Scot,' I said.

'Who?'

'Andrew Scot, one of Maxwell's otter boys.'

Andrew had saved the manuscript of *Raven Seek Thy Brother* from the Sandaig fire and had moved to the island with Maxwell in June 1968.

'He was here at the beginning of the wildlife-park project,' I said. 'There's a photograph in the visitors' centre of him standing in a dinghy off Kyleakin beach throwing an anchor on a line high in the air. You can see the island and cottage in the background. It's a beautiful photograph.'

'Another of Maxwell's boys,' Sandy said.

I've always felt a certain kinship with Andrew Scot. Like me, he had been seduced by Maxwell's books and fallen in love with the idea of living at Sandaig. He'd written fan mail. After Terry Nutkins and Jimmy Watt left Sandaig, Maxwell needed someone to look after the otters, someone to keep him company. Andrew came late to the story. He moved to Sandaig in 1967. In the typescript of *Raven Seek Thy Brother* Maxwell calls him by his real name, Andrew Ball. Andrew changed his surname to 'Scot' when he moved to Scotland.

'They fell out,' I told Sandy. 'An 18-year-old and a dying manic-depressive in his fifties cooped up on the island together. It was bound to happen. They used to fight, really come to blows. He's someone from the books I've never been able to trace.'

'An odd bunch, weren't they?' Sandy said, not really listening. 'Look, can I use this board here? It's a bit big but it'd do.'

'Yes. Whatever you like,' I said. 'I'm going to clean this up and put it in the Long Room. It's a bit of history, a piece of the island's past. Part of the story.'

'Well, whatever. But before you do, here . . . give us a hand with getting this board out, will you?'

≈

There were ten of us on the writers' masterclass – the youngest a gifted teenager from Stornaway, the oldest a septuagenarian ex-teacher from Mull. We read out loud our work, were given writing exercises by a 'facilitator', got drunk and grouched about how unappreciated we were. I went for long Heathcliffian walks along the Cromarty clifftops. One of our number – a poet – had received an Arts Council grant to buy her time to write her debut novel. We all wanted an Arts Council grant. Unlike some of us, the poet had real talent and deserved her award. Another had impressive contacts in the world of Gaelic literature – a tiny, incestuous world, we scoffed. Another had contacts in the world of London publishing, but we thought her writing derivative and dull. We bitched about the 'facilitator' and talked about plot and character and books, books, books. It is a lonesome business, writing books – stuck at a desk in a silent room all day grappling with inarticulacy and never knowing if what you are writing is any good. How can you ever know? It is a fine thing to meet other writers – the only folk who don't think you mad or deluded or odd. It was a grand week.

I'd published guidebooks but that didn't make me an author. Guidebooks don't count. They're compiled rather than written. And I didn't feel like an author. The life of an author was special, and had something to do with acclaim.

I got an hour with the literary agent. I was told right away that *Travels* was too wordy, 'too rich' (meaning turgid and slow). I said I was thinking of writing a comic novel about a dwarf with Asperger's syndrome, set in London and Marrakesh. 'A silly thing,' I offered obsequiously. 'A trashy airport novel, kind of. Think *The Curious Incident of the Dog in the Night-Time* without the maths, crossed with a Paul Bowles novel.'

'I'm not sure that we're quite ready to laugh at dwarves just yet,' said the agent, 'or Asperger's, for that matter.'

'What about a book about hitchhiking around the world on yachts?'

'Um . . . It's not really—'

'Right, well how about this: I grew up in a hippy commune in the Seventies, so it's a book about that.'

'Mmmm . . .' The agent stared at a point on the wall above my head and muttered words that my ears, made deaf by self-delusion and a ton of hope, failed to catch and my mind interpreted as encouragement.

I still like to think that I wasn't the only wannabe author the agent chose not to represent that day.

There was a Glaswegian on the masterclass who had out-thought his roots and gone to live up in the Shetlands – those treeless isles of the far north that lie closer to Norway than to Britain. All the Glaswegian's stories featured road workers hunkered down out of the rain and wind in caravans and sheds on tea breaks, or bending double into gale-force winds and horizontal sleet as they hacked at verges by tarmac roads in the middle of nowhere. They were very funny stories. During our writing exercises I kept hearing a persistent *thud-thud-thud-thud* in the otherwise silent room. It took me a few days to narrow down where it was coming from.

'Have you heard that thudding sound?' I asked the Glaswegian when we were alone.

'Aye, it's me. I've got an artificial heart valve. Made from titanium and Teflon. Lasts forever, I'm told.'

He was about my age. He'd had a heart attack and been declared dead before the medics managed to massage his heart back to life. He'd nearly died again during the open-heart surgery having the valve fitted.

'I guess you don't fear anything any more,' I said. 'Not

after that. You've been to the end of the line, looked over the edge, twice, and come back.'

'You're wrong,' he said. 'I live in constant fear, forever imagining the thudding has stopped. When there's too much noise around me and I can't hear it I start panicking.'

Back on the island I sat at the desk in the bothy and plotted what I should write next. It'd have to be a real sure-fire best-seller. Sometimes Sandy came across with his dog. Exasperated one day by my whining – about being overlooked and rejected, my lack of success, how I'd never be a real author – he told me to forget about it. 'Either try harder, or shut up about it and talk about something else.' As always, he had a point.

≈

In April 1960 Maxwell acquired the male otter, Teko, as a possible mate for Edal. Unfortunately, Edal quickly made it clear that she would kill Teko if given the opportunity (otters are very territorial beasts). Another otter-keeper, besides Jimmy Watt, was required, as the two otters had to be fed, exercised and played with separately. Terry Nutkins, thirteen years old, arrived at Sandaig from London to spend the summer holidays looking after Teko and asked to stay on. Maxwell became Terry's legal guardian.

Ring of Bright Water was published in September 1960 and Gavin Maxwell became hot property, gaining for the first time 'a public'. Readers, the media and his publishers clamoured for more outpourings from his pen, more of the same, and money rolled in. Maxwell's accountant asked him the following year: 'How can I convince you that the *last* thing to do is to earn more money?' A company was created to help defray the heavy tax demands. Electricity was run down the mountain to the house at Sandaig, telephones were installed. From now on Sandaig would be Maxwell's primary residence and the Paultons Square house in London his pied-à-terre and southern office of Gavin Maxwell Enterprises Ltd.

Best-sellerdom brought improvements to Camusfeàrna in the form of heat and light and hot water, where before there had been damp, oil lamps and primus stoves, cold showers in the burn and a trek out into the night to find a place to poo. A Land Rover track was bulldozed to connect the house with the tracks that wound through the fir plantation above. A wooden prefabricated annex was bolted onto the main house to provide bathroom facilities and more rooms. Best-sellerdom bought freezers and big boats and fast vehicles, but it also brought legions of fans (often twenty or more a day) trooping down to Sandaig hoping to meet the famous author and pet his charming otters; which led to the erection of big red 'PRIVATE' signs and barricades, which in turn led to quarrels with the manager of the Eilanreach Estate over Maxwell's increasingly proprietorial attitude towards, and expansion of, Camusfeàrna.

(Maxwell's tenancy agreement included the house and a small section of surrounding land only. Lord Dulverton refused to sell.) Beneath all this activity the idyllic retreat portrayed in *Ring of Bright Water* quickly sank. Perhaps as a reaction to this, Maxwell tried (and failed) to buy the island of Soay again.

An otter chews its food with its needle-like teeth, rather than bolting it as a dog does. Maxwell's first otter, Mij, had been known to nip visitors. The first serious incident involving the Sandaig otters occurred in October 1960 when Edal attacked one of Maxwell's friends. In May 1961 Teko flew into a rage and attacked a visitor. Three months later Edal attacked another visitor and on 27 August she mauled Terry Nutkins's hands so savagely that his middle fingers had to be amputated. More attacks by both otters followed. All had to be hushed up – kept from locals and the press – owing to the adverse publicity it would have caused. After Edal went for Jimmy Watt in January 1962, Maxwell decided the animals could no longer be treated as part of the household and Teko and Edal were confined to their pens at Sandaig. The era of keeping otters as pets was over. It must have been a blow for all concerned – humans and otters alike – but such arrangements often fail. Most wild creatures reared by humans revert to wildness upon reaching maturity, however charming, cuddly and tame they have been as babies. The creatures we more normally call pets – cats and dogs – have taken millennia to domesticate (and even they on occasion show their savage side). But it is a sad irony that Maxwell's otters so soon became chains around his neck. He couldn't get rid of them, for he made his living from them. And they had given him so much.

In 1962, aged forty-seven, Maxwell decided 'to come in from the cold', as he told his future biographer, and get married. Maxwell's bride-to-be, Lavinia Renton (the ex-wife of one of his former SOE colleagues and a daughter of the courtier Sir Alan Lascelles), was a friend of long standing and for a very short while after the wedding it seemed things might work out all right. But the demands of marriage were too much for Maxwell. Lavinia was later to remark: '[Gavin] never grew up . . . Intellectually he was like Sophocles. But emotionally he was like Peter Pan. He had no idea how to cope with the idea of being loved.'*

Maxwell's inability to do the right thing, by his wife and by himself, led to another nervous breakdown and ultimately, and very swiftly – within a few months – to separation and divorce.

By the end of 1962 Maxwell's very cavalier attitude to money meant that he found himself broke again. He bought most things on tick, keeping accounts with tailors and boot makers as well as butchers and garages; he lived

---

* Botting, p. 395.

high on the hog and never kept track of his spending. He provided generously for the boys at Sandaig, but he built up a complicated empire and staffed it with teenagers (never the most reliable age group). Projects fell behind schedule, debts remained unsettled. He spent the winters ranging across North Africa and preferred it to be believed by all but his inner circle that he was always away, so he could never be called to account. Michael Cuddy, the young secretary of Gavin Maxwell Enterprises Ltd, composed letters to fans, associations, creditors and lawyers replete with excuses and delaying tactics. Maxwell was always 'in the North', 'abroad', 'uncontactable'. Maxwell remained on the move, spending, leaving his charmed minions to pick up the pieces in his wake. Kathleen Raine wrote in *The Lion's Mouth*: 'Gavin had another quality which likewise owed, no doubt, to his birth: he had the gift of making us all his slaves. It came naturally to Gavin to initiate adventure, and to assign the parts to those who gladly joined him.'

Adolescents, naturally, refuse to remain in aspic. They mature, tend to resent attempts by parents (including adoptive parents) to control them, and they will inevitably want to fly the nest. Terry Nutkins left Maxwell's employ in 1963. He told Maxwell's biographer:

I never played at Camusfeàrna. I was never a boy [there]. From the moment I got on that night train

[from London to go up to Sandaig] my life was serious
. . . And yet I had so much . . .

Life wasn't easy – the isolation, the ruggedness of it, all
those rucksacks up and down the hill in the rain. There
were days when I was absolutely fed up. I used to look
at the ships going by down the Sound of Sleat and
the scattered houses far away on Skye, and I'd think:
'They're all with their families and we haven't got anything.' There was an emptiness there, and I used to
love it when people came to stay.

But I am grateful to Gavin in many ways. I had a life
unlike any other boy in Britain, Jimmy excepted.

After Terry left Sandaig, a series of teenagers was engaged
to help Jimmy, but none stayed long. Jimmy Watt stayed
(he would eventually leave in 1966), looking after the
provisioning and maintenance of the household, the two
otters, the assorted vehicles, the boats, and Maxwell when
he was there. If you look closely at the photographs in the
Camusfeàrna books, Jimmy's hands are more often than
not covered in oil. They remind me of Master Dip the
Dyer's son's hands in the Happy Families card game;
Maxwell's hands, by comparison, are always immaculate,
almost manicured.

Maxwell alighted at Sandaig between travels, and
returned there to write the second book in his Camusfeàrna trilogy, *The Rocks Remain*, in a little over a month.

The book, like its predecessor, was a best-seller on both sides of the Atlantic and Maxwell used some of the proceeds to buy the two lighthouse keepers' cottages at Ornsay and Kyleakin. Richard Frere carried out the necessary alteration and renovation of the cottages and his wife, Joan, designed the interiors. The idea was to rent them out to holidaymakers.

In June 1963 Maxwell rolled his Land Rover near Glenelg and as the car turned over, his left foot became jammed in the pedals. Extricating himself, Maxwell managed to damage some blood vessels in his foot so severely that the blood flow became impaired and his foot started to die. In October 1963, while undergoing an operation (a lumbar sympathectomy) to repair the damage, Maxwell caught a hospital bug, which led to further operations and a prolonged period of convalescence. He was incapable of walking far for months afterwards and spent the summer of 1964 lame and housebound at Sandaig, working on two books simultaneously: a memoir of his childhood, *The House of Elrig*, and *Lords of the Atlas*, a book charting the rise and fall of a Moroccan Berber dynasty, the House of Glaoui.

A spectre from the past dragged Maxwell further into debt in 1965 when an action for libel was brought against him and his publishers by an Italian involved in the events Maxwell had written about in *God Protect Me from My Friends*, his 1956 book about the Sicilian bandit Salvatore

Giuliano. Maxwell lost the case and was ordered to pay damages as well as costs on both sides.

That August the directors of Gavin Maxwell Enterprises Ltd convened to discuss Maxwell's finances (i.e. his debt crisis) and recommended that the two lighthouse keepers' cottages be sold, Teko and Edal sent to a zoo, and Sandaig, which was reckoned to be costing the company £7,000 a year to run, closed down. Maxwell's answer was, predictably, non-contrite and wayward. He fired his office manager, Michael Cuddy, installed himself as Managing Director of the company and sold the lease of the Paultons Square house.

Money *was* coming in from the publication of *The House of Elrig*, the rental of the lighthouse keepers' cottages, sales of previous books and Maxwell's other literary pursuits, but nowhere near enough to discharge his debts. It wasn't just that Maxwell's spending was out of control; it had never been under control – ever. He was in hock to everyone, including his publishers, and the chickens had finally come home to roost. Creditors pressed for payment. Then Maxwell played his masterstroke. He invited Richard Frere to take over the running of Gavin Maxwell Enterprises Ltd. What he was offering Frere was the managing directorship of a bankrupt company whose sole purpose was to fund the spendthrift pirouettes of a chaotic, manic-depressive genius.

Richard Frere must have been as extraordinary a figure

as Gavin Maxwell, for he accepted and set to, it seems, with relish, gradually extracting the company from the quagmire of bills and unpaid invoices. (An Englishman who'd transplanted to the Highlands for, at first, the climbing, Frere wrote several books about his life in the Highlands and led an extremely active and varied life.)

By the time Jimmy Watt left Sandaig in May 1966, Maxwell had been obliged to come to terms with the recommendations of his company directors, and perhaps he felt that Sandaig – Camusfeàrna – had died with the departure of Jimmy. He agreed for Sandaig to be closed down and the otters sent to a zoo.

In July 1966, at a low ebb, Maxwell went to stay at his brother Aymer's house on the Greek island of Euboea. By chance Kathleen Raine was holidaying at a friend's house nearby. Raine had been writing a memoir, *The Lion's Mouth*. Much of it was about her love for Maxwell, part of it told of the curse she had laid upon the rowan tree at Sandaig all those years ago. One evening Raine and Maxwell met and – strange motives – she gave him her manuscript to read.

The otter attacks, the disastrous marriage, his car crash and lameness, his maladies both mental and physical, the chaos of his life, the crucifying debt, Terry's departure and Jimmy's wish to break away from his mentor, the end of the Sandaig idyll . . . Maxwell wouldn't be the first to look for someone else to blame for personal misfortunes.

That winter he decamped to Tangier for six months and wrote, in my opinion, his best book – *Raven Seek Thy Brother*.

≈

The Bright Water Visitors' Centre reopened for the Easter school holidays. One of the trustees took over the running of the Centre and John the chairman got down to some serious form-filling. Applications for funding were completed and posted and we all waited for various august committees to meet, deem the Kyleakin Lighthouse Island Trust worthy, and then send large cheques.

I revised my tour-guide spiel, donned my binoculars and waited at the gate at 2 p.m. every other day for visitors. Pete and I continued to take it in turns to lead the tours. A succession of holidaymakers came to spend a week in the cottage. In the evenings I retired to my room and half-listened to their conversations coming through the walls, the tumbling of pots and pans in the kitchen, their laughter and, sometimes, singing.

People came to the island with their stories, adding pieces to the jigsaw – a man who'd acquired Maxwell's old Mercedes 300SL Roadster (registration plate number: HOT32) and had stored it away ('It's gathering dust in my lock-up, a restoration project, but you know, these things, they take time.'); people came by who had known Maxwell, others who'd heard stories about him: that he'd sired a son by a crofter on Knoydart, that he'd been blackmailed out of a fortune after some homosexual entanglement, that he was bad with animals, negligent, evil ('That bloody man! He was a cruel, rude bastard,' one woman from the village spat). A Canadian visitor told me stories of spending the summer of 1970 working for Alexander, the man who bought the island after Maxwell's death, ferrying tourists across from Kyleakin Beach in a leaky rowing boat to the miniature zoo they'd created. I heard rumours (there were always rumours) that Jimmy and Terry didn't get on – that there had been jealousy because Maxwell had chosen Jimmy and not Terry as his legal heir, that Terry had gone on to inherit a fortune from Johnny Morris, his co-presenter on the long-running children's TV show *Animal Magic*, that Jimmy was a kind and gentle man, that he was a bad man. Visitors came, we stood in the sun and looked down the loch and mused, reflected on life.

Pete Baggeley was a natural tour guide. He was also the treasurer of the Kyleakin Lighthouse Island Trust, Secretary of the Skye Terrier Association, a member of the Pteridological Society (ferns), sat on the boards of several 'Important Organizations' (Pete's words, not mine) and was the Secretary of the Kyleakin Community Council. Pete was the archetypal interfering Incomer. He and his wife had moved up to Skye five years before from Hertfordshire, where he'd worked as an engineer until he'd retired. He knew that his generosity of spirit was often abused by the Natives but carried on giving anyway, because for Pete nothing was worse than having nothing to do. He was Sandy's opposite in this respect. Sandy had all the time in the world, Pete had almost none.

After he'd led a tour he'd come and find me wherever I was on the island and he'd find fault with whatever it was I was doing. He'd pour scorn on the Trust or the government, or run down a Local he'd decided was a waste of space, and then he'd tell me the News:

'There's been a terrorist attack on the London Underground. Seven hundred injured and thirty-eight dead at the last count. Four bombs: King's Cross, Edgware Road, Liverpool Street and a double-decker bus in Tavistock Road. It's terrible!'

'They've discovered a new planet circling the sun beyond Pluto. Incredible!'

'The police have shot dead an innocent Brazilian man on the Tube in London. They had him down as a suicide bomber. Idiots!'

'Kyleakin Bonfire Night has been cancelled because of new health-and-safety regulations. We just can't afford the safety measures they're demanding. There goes another tradition!'

'I heard you were blotto in the King's Arms the other evening. Drunkard!'

'Who's that young woman I've seen you knocking about with? Dark horse!'

'Come and visit us.'

≈

Maxwell returned to Britain from Morocco in the early summer of 1967, coughing up blood. He had picked up an intestinal malady in North Africa, and exploratory tests showed a clot on a lung. While he'd been away, negotiations to send Edal and Teko to Aberdeen Zoo had fallen through, as had another plan to send them to Woburn Abbey Safari Park. But a visit to Sandaig by the American film director Jack Couffer set in train the making of the 1969 movie of *Ring of Bright Water*, which would star Bill Travers and Virginia McKenna. Meanwhile, Richard Frere had found a buyer for the Ornsay lighthouse cottage, and 17-year-old Andrew Scot had been employed to look after the otters down at Sandaig.

By the winter of 1967 money was coming in from various sources and Frere was able to settle many of the company's accounts. Andrew Scot was proving to be an able and practical employee and an intelligent companion, and had initiated the release of Teko and Edal from their zoo-like confinement in the enclosures at Sandaig. Richard Frere was a hands-on, competent manager of Gavin Maxwell Enterprises Ltd and *Raven Seek Thy Brother*, scheduled for publication the following year, would bring in more money. It seemed that things were looking up for Gavin Maxwell. He must have wondered if the curse had finally run its course.

≈

In the mountains surrounding me the cuckoos sang their lonesome lament. By May, while the daffodils were wilting on the lawn, the rest of the island had turned on the Technicolor. There was the puce of the rhododendrons, the bright yellow of the gorse, the orange and yellow of the 'bacon-and-eggs' bird's-foot trefoil; purpley-blue self-heal, pink dog-rose, violets, pendulous near-scarlet foxgloves, white blossom on the rowans, the delicate yellows of tormentil. Dandelions and white clover were everywhere. The willowy stems of the fireweed grew chest-high and the sea pinks – 'thrift' – bloomed on the lichen-covered rocks by the sea. The ash trees were already decked out in green and the reed beds were full of flowers. Variegated, multi-hued caterpillars looped and butterflies danced, whitethroats flashed as they flew at each other and sparred above the brambles by the bothy; greenfinches and dun-nocks and chaffinches flickered as they fought for territory and mates. Whirling, diving, hovering, squabbling gulls descended on floating islets of dense weed to peck at the baby moon jellyfish and larvae and tiny crabs that shel-tered within. At night in the dark, with the sea warm enough for phosphorescence, I watched porpoises and dolphins switchback and dart like sparkling torpedoes.

Before the coming of the bridge, a narrow channel ran between Kyleakin Lighthouse Island and a nearby, much smaller, island. The bridge-builders filled in this channel and the two islands are now one, but the engineers also laid three dwarf-diameter concrete pipes so that the island's otters could continue to follow the path of the old channel between the loch and the open sea. These concrete pipes beneath the approach road, these otter underpasses, are much used, not only by otters but also by sneaky fishermen sheltering from the rain, the odd cat, and a warden called Dan. And it is on the open-sea side of the island – the north-west – where, if you are very quiet, and if the wind is blowing from the right direction, and if you sit very still and wait forever, you will most often see otters. There are freshwater pools on the north-west side. It is quiet and hidden from the road by thick gorse bushes and a stone wall; there are few paths on the wilder side of the island away from the house. The otters have slides and rolling places and holts here; areas of flattened grass and well-trodden otter paths lead into secret places under the bracken and heather, and on little bluffs looking out to sea you will come across crunched-up crab carapaces and langoustine claws, and spraint.

One sunshine and sunglasses day, clambering round the

shoreline, I came to one of the otter underpasses and saw fresh spraint on a rock at its entrance. I knelt and examined it. Urine around the spraint was still dribbling down from the rock. It was very fresh spraint. I stood up, and spotted a splodge on a nearby boulder. I hopped over to inspect it. A paw print. There was a dark, wet slash too – the mark of an otter's tail – near the splodge. I looked for more paw prints and found one, then another, and another. I must be only a minute or two behind an oblivious otter. I couldn't believe my luck. I scanned the rocks ahead of me. A little whiplike tail, held high, was moving away from me among the rocks. The whip disappeared, reappeared. I set off, hopping as quietly as I could, and carefully, from boulder to slippery boulder.

I stopped, wobbled, looked up and an otter was looking straight back at me.

'Peep!'

The face disappeared. I hopped to where the otter had been. Paw prints disappeared down the steep filigreed shoreline into the sea. I settled myself into the rocks and scanned my binoculars back and forth across the sea. Gulls circled and seals lounged on the beaches like fat slugs. Out on the brown-and-bone skerries piebald oystercatchers skittered and stopped, skittered and stopped. Otters are the commandos, the SAS, of the animal world, and the one I sought had vanished.

≈

Afflicted as I was by a preposterous nostalgia for a way of life I'd never known, rather than stroll over the bridge to visit the shops or friends in the villages, I'd go by boat. The lighthouse keepers and Maxwell and Richard Frere and all the others had to go by boat when my almost-isle had been a proper island, and so would I. But to do so involved far more than a mere short jog down to the slip, a gazelle-like leap into my dinghy and away. Oh ho-ho!

1. I had to collect the oars and the lifejacket from the bothy and convey these down to the slip (stuffing the lifejacket into a safe place among the rocks if it happened to be blustery).

2. A trip back up the slipway, past the cottage, up the steps to the bothy, check that the fuel tank on the *Seagull* was full,* lug the Seagull (an *all-metal* outboard, not one of the lightweight plastic-cased jobs – heavy) onto my shoulder, grab the can of spare fuel (just in case), lock the bothy door, trundle down the steps, trip past the cottage and down to the slip. Lay all this gear down.

3. Pull the dinghy up against the slip from its mooring out in Lighthouse Bay and tie the painter off on one of the slipway mooring rings.

---

* Fill if necessary.

4. (*a*) Juggle the oars, lifejacket and fuel can into the boat and clamber aboard. (*b*) Haul in the Seagull. (*c*) Fit the clamp of the Seagull onto the transom and tighten the wing nuts (very important).

5. Climb back out of the boat onto the slip and untie the painter from the mooring ring. Pull the dinghy broadside to the slip and leap aboard like a professional boat-handler pirate.*

6. Release the aft mooring line from the mooring buoy in the bay, fit the oars . . .

7. (a) Then go boating, or (b) tie up the boat again, trudge back up to the house/bothy once more to collect whatever it was I'd forgotten, and then go boating.

Depending on the state of the tide and the direction of the wind, the dinghy could be riding the waves on its mooring far out in the middle of Lighthouse Bay, or aground. Low tide made things a little easier as I could just walk out into the emptied-out bay to sling all the gear in the boat. However, I then had to heave the lead-heavy dinghy around hefty lumps of rock and over ankle-twisting hardcore left over from the bridge-building to reach sea.

And I felt very vulnerable down there beneath the bridge. Sometimes kids, thirty metres above me, watched

---

* Yeah, right.

me for a while and then, just for fun, lobbed stones. The setup wasn't ideal, and it made me realize how time-consuming and inconvenient life on the island must have been when it was a proper island. Winters, especially, can't have been easy.

After Johnny Ach's funeral, several boxes of files relating to the Kyleakin Lighthouse Island Trust were cleared from his office and taken to the Bright Water Visitors' Centre. I asked the trustees if I could go through them. Among the papers was a letter written by Richard Frere to Virginia McKenna – 'After the house at Sandaig burnt down, Gavin was a shadow of his former self. He put a brave face on it, but he was lost, and he had lost almost everything . . . the fire destroyed all that he owned. In some sense, perhaps, the fire also destroyed him' – and a memorandum that had been sent to Johnny Ach marked 'Private and Confidential'. Since this didn't relate to the Trust in any way I decided to mail it back to the person who had sent it – Jimmy Watt.

Waves were crowding up the loch and pounding onto rocks when I set out in the dinghy for the post office, but I'd been lurking in my room for most of the day and a challenge would do me good and clear my head. I had pulled on waterproofs, loaded up the dinghy and locked up.

The dinghy rolled around once we were out of the shelter of the slip and the wind pushed us under the bridge and out towards the Inner Sound. I struggled with the starter cord before managing to get it wrapped around the flywheel, fire up the Seagull and set a course east for the pontoons by the Lochalsh Hotel in Kyle. Waves smashed into the bow of the boat and slopped over the sides; spray blew into my face. I slowed the revs and the boat cut a more comfortable path through the choppy, sloppy water. I looked about me. Mine was the only boat moving along the loch. A couple of yachts were moored to the pontoons ahead. A fishing boat was tied to a mooring buoy, its bow dipping into oncoming waves like a nodding donkey.

The wind coming straight off the Kintail hills was icy and I was quickly feeling its chill. I pushed the throttle forward hard and a *ker-lunk!* bumped the steady blatter of the Seagull into a high-pitched whine. The dinghy slowed and bounced about in the waves. I cut the engine, wrapped the starter cord around the flywheel and yanked. There was that hysterical whining again, no churning of water, no bubbles or eddies behind the boat. The propeller had sheared off. I cut the engine. It had failed me yet again. The dinghy bounced and swung broadside to oncoming waves. More sea slopped in. Spray from the crests of waves flew into my face and on down the loch. We were in danger of getting flipped. I grabbed the oars and rowed. The wind blew. The waves threatened. I rowed, rowed, rowed towards the pitching, rolling pontoons, rocking on their anchors. Incrementally the warmth and security of the

Lochalsh Hotel bar came closer. I focussed and hauled on the oars, keeping the bow of the boat just off the waves, and by the time I got the painter around a cleat in the lee of the pontoons the sweat running down my back was running cold.

The walk to the post office, where I mailed a very damp letter to Jimmy Watt, warmed me slightly; the Guinness and whisky chasers I downed in the Lochalsh Hotel warmed me more and whether by merry design or drunken chance, my plucky little boat and I practically surfed all the way back home to the island. I had to row like crazy to prevent us being blown under the bridge and out into the boiling cauldron of the Inner Sound, but as ever the drink had a calming influence on us both and saved the day (better to roll with it than fight it). On reflection, though, thinking about it, I could have just walked back.

The Seagull's injuries were terminal. According to Sandy, the fact that any engine works at all, ever, is a miracle, because all the constituent parts of a machine are always degrading. All that any human-made 'thing' ever wants to do is break itself down and return to its elemental state. As ever, Sandy has a point.

≈

The island gave up another of its secrets one May afternoon while I was out walking the shoreline looking for otters. It was a day of sunshine and showers – the sun shining strongly to dry the island before another rogue black cloud came to douse it again. I was scrambling up a bank below the lighthouse wall when one of these clouds happened to pass overhead and a light rain began to fall. As I hauled myself up past a smooth patch of rock, letters gradually appeared on it like a message in invisible ink declaring itself. I looked closer at the rock and rubbed rain across it.

J. CURRIE

I went to the bothy and pulled the copy of the Lighthouse Keepers' Register from the filing cabinet.

'Mr John Currie,' I read, 'Assistant Keeper, 18 January 1872–8 November 1880. Left Kyleakin for Dunnethead Lighthouse by John o'Groats. Period of service at Kyleakin Light: 7¾ years.'

I imagined John Currie then, pictured him in my mind's eye, 120-odd years ago, sitting alone on that sheltered spot down by the lighthouse, hidden by the wall from the Principal keeper's beady eye. Mr J. Currie has a view out to Raasay and Pabay and the other islands from there, over to the Cuillin Hills and Skye. Perhaps he is watching one of the blazing sunsets, or pondering his future, his love, his life, before carving his name to leave his mark on the island where he's been living for so long. Seven years and three quarters. Is it a long time?

After discovering John Currie's graffiti I often inspected it on my rounds, and it became a talking point on my tours.

On very dry days or when it was wet, you couldn't see anything there at all. It needed a *soupçon* of water and no more for John Currie to appear. I pointed it out to Marcus and he made a polite noise in the back of his throat and, like John the chairman and Pete, nodded politely before moving the conversation onto other things. But when I showed Mr Currie's graffiti to Sandy he peered at it for ages. Then he knelt and ripped away some of the moss surrounding it.

'No. Nothing more,' he said. 'It's a shame there's no date or anything. But that's magical, Dan, really wonderful. What else have you found?'

So I showed him the self-winding watch (broken) I'd found on a wall under bracken by one of the paths. And the *Daily Record* newspaper from Wednesday, 12 June 1953 that I'd fished out from under the bench in the lighthouse shed. And the collection of old-fashioned glass bottles I'd gathered from the seaweed and slime on the beaches on the lowest of low spring tides. I showed him the old medicine bottles and pieces of pottery, the lighthouse keepers' cap-badge all green with verdigris, which I'd pulled from the sea; and the brass twelve-sided thrupenny bit (1966; still in use when Gavin Maxwell was living on the island) I'd found in Teko's shed. I told him about the pair of ancient leather hiking boots and the Welsh love spoon I'd found; about the rusting poles and rotting netting on the site of the wildlife park aviary behind the cottage. I took

him to the ash tree by the Sensory Garden and pointed out
the glass bottle tied to a branch (a wind chime? a house for
wasps?). We crept around the shoreline and I pointed out
the otters' holts and crouches and rolling sites, their slides
and laying-up places. We examined the low stone founda-
tions of a building that had once stood at the bottom of
the lawn in front of the house (a privy?) and the old jetty
(where cinders from decades of lighthouse keepers' fires
still showed beneath the turf), and a fork, engraved with
the Northern Lighthouse Board's initials, melded to a
rock in East Bay. I showed him the enigmatic white lines
painted on the roof of a little cave near the otter underpasses, and the white crosses painted one above the other
on a rock on the north-west side of the island (leading
lines to guide fishing boats around an obstruction in the
shallows nearby?). I shared with him the photos I'd found
in the bothy filing cabinet, and the drawings and paintings
and old letters.

'You've explored it all,' Sandy said.

'I know every inch,' I said. 'I'm in love with it.'

'Good for you,' Sandy said. 'Good for you.'

Six

SECOND SUMMER

I loved pretty much everything about my job on the island, but there was one aspect of it I didn't love, and which often I found myself avoiding.

Imagine you are up on the bridge. From there you can see the network of paths, the lighthouse and the lighthouse shed, the heather-thatch roofs of the hide, the cottage, the bothy, the cobbled path, the slipway, and my little dinghy moored to its buoy in the bay. It all looks rather intriguing. If you were to stand in front of that cottage, you could get a fantastic photograph of the loch and the Kintail hills beyond.

Wouldn't it be nice to get a closer look at the lighthouse and examine the great span of the bridge from beneath? And what *are* those little buildings that look like African huts? What a place to kick back, take in the view, sink a few beers, even smoke a joint maybe. You've heard a famous writer used to own the island, and a man in the village told you there are otters. You've always wanted to see an otter.

There *may* be someone living in the house, but would they *really* mind if you just had a quick look around? You wouldn't be long. And perhaps they're away anyway. Perhaps the cottage is just another holiday home like so many other cottages around here. So you saunter back down off the bridge and nip over the wall onto the island.

Or imagine you're a Native who visited the island as a child, who knew the lighthouse keepers and their families, who once fished off the rocks here and explored; imagine how galling it must have been to look on as the lighthouse keepers left and strangers came and erected their 'Keep Off' and 'Private Property' signs. It is ironic that after the auctioning off of the island was stopped to save it from falling into the hands of yet another 'my home is my castle so keep off' outsider, one of the first edicts issued by the Kyleakin Lighthouse Island Trust was that 'access to the "community resource" must be controlled to safeguard the wildlife and plants on the island'. Today only *paying* visitors – accompanied by a warden – are permitted on the island. How typical it is of the Highlands and Hebrides that the new 'owners' of the island are, in the main, strangers, incomers from that crowded country to the south.

And so it is not surprising that Natives and Locals feel no inclination to support the Kyleakin Lighthouse Island Trust. They were locked out from the beginning. I could never see where the 'community resource' came into it.

Kyleakin Lighthouse Island remains, in all but name, a private island.

As warden I had to deal with the fallout of all this and it was horrible. Anyone prepared to clamber over the otter wall is prepared to brazen it out. Some of the interlopers were shameless – marching about the island, video camera in hand, making themselves comfortable on the bench in front of the house. Cockle-pickers came to fill their sacks at low tide; parties of kayakers used the beaches to picnic and pee. Some climbed onto the island to make a point. A gang of cast fishermen from Skye got angry when I approached them, sick of being told to clear off their ancestral lands by Incomers like me. I routinely came across stubbed-out joints and empty beer cans in all the prettiest spots on the wilder side of the island away from the house.

Almost nobody meant any harm. Most were merely curious. They had no interest in the history of the island and wanted a quick look-see, not a guided tour. But to confront was part of my job. So I confronted, trembling gently, pretending I was some kind of an authority figure.

I always hoped the trustees might open the island to all, for free. I *wanted* crowds on the island exploring and picnicking. I liked the idea of happy screaming inquisitive kids running around, bringing the island alive. Then in my mind's eye I'd see the detritus that humans leave behind: lazily dropped litter, empty bottles and crushed cans and

crisp packets and dog mess; the damage that bored teenagers do; break-ins and thefts. A month before my arrival
on the island teenagers had vaulted the wall and had a
party in the hide. One of the gang had scrawled on the
wall:

05/05/05

Duncan Huckle* wuz ere!!!

Shagged Kelly Maclean† all nite!!

It hadn't taken too much detective work to hunt down
the lad (and lass) responsible for this outrage, but the
damage had been done. A trustee screwed locks onto all
the windows of the hide and from then on the island was
locked down at night.

During my second summer I was awoken at dawn one
Saturday by the sound of footsteps on the gravel outside
the house. There were no guests staying in the cottage and
none expected, especially at that hour. I heard the handle
of the half-windowed door of my room being turned and
looked on, wide awake now, as the curtain was slowly
pushed aside and the face of a young woman peered in. I
sat up on one elbow.

'Oh!' she said, seeing me. 'I'm so sorry.' She had an
English, public-school accent. Perhaps she slurred a little.

---

* Not his real name.

† Not her real name, either.

I stared at her. Blinked.

'I . . . I couldn't help it,' she said. 'I was curious.'

There was nothing to say. It was five o'clock in the morning.

'I'm sorry,' she said. 'Good . . . night.' The pretty head withdrew, the curtain slowly fell back into place and the door was gently pulled to.

Now, however pretty you are, however full of post-party *joie de vivre*, would *you* wander into someone's garden, have a poke around, a little sit down and, oh what the heck . . . see if there's a way into the house for a bit of a nose around? To my mind there's a bold black division line between curiosity and housebreaking.

The Trust's fear that too many visitors would damage the ecology of the island, drive away the otters and scare away the birds seems to me unrealistic. Nature is far more resilient than we think. And otters are all over the West Highlands and in many places take little notice of their human neighbours. Otters brought up a litter of cubs beneath a pair of dilapidated wooden lifeboats that for years lay beside the frenetically busy car park in Kyle. Otters negotiate the ladders of Kyle Quay to get to the fish on trawlers and they are regularly seen on the pontoons in Kyleakin.

Trusts tend to be conservative bodies and trustees wary of and resistant to change. It will take a fearless set of trustees to abolish the ruling of controlled access, but until the island is opened up, local antipathy towards the island and the Trust is likely to remain.

≈

A trustee telephoned to say that John Lister-Kaye was coming to the island. He would be arriving with students from his Aigas Field Centre. The group were especially keen to see otters and Lister-Kaye would be bringing with him an object that in Maxwell's day had sat on the mantelpiece in the Long Room. I asked the trustee if she expected me to magic otters into view. 'Do what you can,' she said.

In the summer of 1969 Maxwell invited Lister-Kaye, then a budding young naturalist, to act as curator and manager of the proposed island wildlife park and help him put together a book on British mammals he'd been commissioned to write. The plan was to make the island a tourist attraction. Maxwell would then be able to collect a mass of material for another book, and the income from the wildlife park would save him from having to write a book a year, as he'd been doing since the publication of *Ring of Bright Water*. Maxwell, for all his creative ability, is said to have loathed writing. He was getting older, was frequently in poor health and was keen to escape the demands of the desk, his publisher, and his readership.

By the time Lister-Kaye arrived, Andrew Scot had left Maxwell's employ and another school-leaver, Donald

Mitchell, had taken his place. Lister-Kaye worked on the British Mammals book and took charge of the wildlife-park project, supervising the erection of pens and aviaries and helping Donald Mitchell look after the assortment of animals that Maxwell and his contacts were collecting and installing on the island.

When Maxwell died only a few months later, in September 1969, the wildlife-park project was abandoned. Lister-Kaye moved to a cottage elsewhere in the Highlands and over the winter wrote a book, *The White Island*, about his few months working for Maxwell. Afterwards, he stayed on in the Highlands and established one of the first eco-tourism ventures – taking visitors on trips up into the hills to identify the flora and fauna they found there. For a time Richard Frere, an experienced mountaineer, had worked for the company. Later, Lister-Kaye married and bought a semi-derelict country house and estate in Inverness-shire, where he established the Aigas Field Centre and ran courses for aspiring naturalists and environmentalists.

Pete and I stood beneath the rowan tree by the gate. I was looking forward to welcoming a past inhabitant back to the island. Pete had elected to escort the group. From where we stood in the morning sunshine we could look across to Kyleakin Beach. Brightly coloured cagoules were gathered around a tall man with a walking stick. A white minibus was parked in the car park behind them. Pete and I watched the group climb into the minibus and the minibus pass down the Kyleakin road before disappearing behind the trees where the German girl had once pitched her tent. A few minutes later the minibus pulled up beside us and an upright, well-built, balding man climbed down from the passenger seat clutching a thumbstick. He wore a well-tailored country suit. A pair of binoculars was slung around his neck. He smiled confidently at Pete and me as he strolled through the gate, held out a hand and introduced himself. I noticed a signet ring on the little finger of his left hand.

'And my students,' he said, waving an arm at the cagoule-wearers piling out of the minibus, 'are just *desperate* to see otters!'

Once the students had gathered around us I closed the gate and Pete led us all down to the house and into the Long Room, where he spoke about the history of the island and Gavin Maxwell. When Pete had come to the end of his spiel, Lister-Kaye coughed politely and told us he wished to say a few words. We stood in silence on the faded Moroccan rug. Lister-Kaye reached into the pocket of his jacket and withdrew, with a flourish, a blue spotted handkerchief.

'I remember this room very well,' he informed us. 'We spent a lot of time in here – Gavin and I, Jimmy Watt, Donald Mitchell – sitting beside the fire, drinking Gavin's very good whisky, discussing everything under the sun. Virginia McKenna has done a good job of recreating the

ambience of the Long Room, except it was always much
more untidy, and smelly. I remember the ghastly stench
and the mess on the carpet after Teko had finished mark-
ing it as his territory, and the time we had a gannet in
here that shat, copiously, everywhere. In fact,' Lister-Kaye
declared, looking down and tapping a brogue on the rug,
'this carpet has survived remarkably well!

'Gavin smoked like a chimney – up to eighty cigarettes
a day, and the whole house reeked of smoke when he was
here. There were ashtrays in every room, even beside the
lavatory and bathtub. And he wasn't very domestic – there
was always a pile of washing-up waiting for someone to do
it. Sadly, Gavin was gravely ill while I was living here and
he was away a lot, visiting relatives, and later in hospital in
Inverness. Donald and I were mostly here alone with the
animals Gavin had obtained; his two whacking great deerhounds, and Teko. But I like to think that I came to know
him well, and I will always be grateful to him for what he
gave me.'

Lister-Kaye unravelled the spotted handkerchief he'd
been holding and produced a jagged piece of beige rock
about the size of a boy's fist. He held the rock up for us all
to see, a cluster of sharp-edged discs, resembling the petals
of a flower.

'This is a desert rose. Gavin had a small collection of
these that he'd brought back from his trips to North Africa
and scattered around the house. They are created by

gypsum particles crystallizing beneath the sand of the Sahara Desert. After Gavin died I took this piece to remember him by. I've kept it with me these past thirty-six years, but it belongs here, on the mantelpiece, in this wonderful room.'

Lister-Kaye passed the desert rose to Pete to the sound of applause.

'Now, let's go and look at otters,' Lister-Kaye said.

We followed Pete to the hide. I stood outside in the hot sun while the students gathered in the hide to peer through binoculars at seals basking on the skerries and seabirds flying and floating over the bright blue Inner Sound. Lister-Kaye came out from the cold gloom of the hide and stood beside me. He blotted out the sun. I put my binoculars to my eyes, searching for otters for the students.

'Donald and I used to go out fishing by those skerries,' Lister-Kaye said.

I removed the binoculars from my eyes and stepped back a little to stand again in the sun.

'There wasn't much money so we were always looking for ways to feed the animals for free. We caught a lot of Teko's food out there – saithe and lythe.'

'What was he like, Gavin?' I said.

After a moment, Lister-Kaye said: 'He was incredibly fatalistic.'

'Perhaps he'd picked it up in North Africa,' I said, 'or when he was in Iraq. Muslims believe everything is ordained. *Maktoub*, they say – "It is written". They believe our lives have already been mapped out by God, before we're born, and there's nothing we can do about it.'

Lister-Kaye narrowed his eyes. 'Gavin would say to me, "It's all going *too* well, John, *too* well. It can't last!"'

I said, 'Eighty cigarettes a day works out to be around one cigarette every ten minutes. Is it really possible to smoke that many in a day?'

There was a silence. I put my binoculars to my eyes again.

'You see, there just wasn't the medical knowledge or the technology available in the late sixties. By the time the specialists found the shadows on Gavin's lungs it was far too late. He was a brave man in many ways. But a fatalist.'

I lowered my bins and was about to say something or other but Lister-Kaye had put his to his eyes and was looking out to sea. Lowering them, he caught sight of a butterfly blundering by and called to a student who had come to stand near us, 'A painted lady, Giles. *Vanessa cardui*. They migrate en masse from the Atlas Mountains of Morocco. Quite a rarity, this far north.'

'Ah,' said Giles. 'What about otters, though?'

Pete's snort came from the cool gloom of the hide. 'Otters're around,' he was telling the students inside, 'but I rarely see them on a tour. I often see them in the evenings down by the river. Everybody thinks they're rare but they're everywhere up here.'

No otters were seen that day, and after Lister-Kaye and his students left, and after Pete had driven back over the bridge trailing a cloud of oily smoke behind him, I felt unsettled. A ghost had come back to the island, only to leave me wandering alone in a museum again. I locked up and walked down the slip to my dinghy, cast off and went for a long row around the island, then headed further out to the neighbouring islands and skerries, pulling hard on the oars.

As I passed between the skerries where John Lister-Kaye and Donald Mitchell had once fished, seals lolloped and splashed into the sea from their basking spots and came bobbing round the boat. They eyed me, curious dogs, blowing bubbles. Then they sank without a sound below the surface, leaving only rings in the still, bright water, and these rings expanded and became eclipsed by the greater expanse of the sea, leaving only bubbles, like memories, behind.

≈

Memories of that second summer return: a male blackbird singing, late afternoon, on the uppermost branch of a dead wind-burnt tree beside the bothy; a hedge sparrow hopping along the path under hanging locks of honeysuckle; a wood mouse, watched from the half-windowed door one quiet afternoon, idling down the path before disappearing under a rose bush, reappearing for an instant, then lifting high its back legs and wading gamely into the jungly grass behind the house; a party of knots, curlews and ten purple sandpipers dipping their long thin beaks into the mud and seaweed of an exposed shoreline; the sun breaking through a grey sky and a big dog otter with white bib catching crabs in East Bay before swimming out of view towards the underpass; arctic skuas – dark brown and falconesque – swooping into the Inner Sound to mob and harry terns and gulls into giving up whatever prize morsel they'd foraged; bats quartering overhead by the lighthouse in the gloaming.

Moon jellyfish – full-size now – and the occasional lion's mane jellyfish washed up on the beaches. The bramble bushes and rushes became spotted with cuckoo spit, and that second summer the paths were edged with wild grasses. Common blue and Scotch argus butterflies floated and fluttered around the wild roses and foxgloves, and all around the island scarlet and green velvet six-spot burnet moths clung in couples in amorous posture. From the open water of the Inner Sound came the creaky-kneed growl of the puffins – those little men with harlequin beaks and sad-eyed mien. Flocks of guillemots and razorbills sped and turned under the bridge and over the island. The common and black-headed and herring gulls busied about in a marauding, raucous mob. The flowers of bell heather turned the surrounding mountainsides the colour of blackcurrant coulis.

And there were mysteries: at three o'clock in the afternoon, during a tour, a roe deer (the same make as Bambi) comes bounding through the chest-high bracken in front of the hide from the direction of the lighthouse, veers away when it sees us and leaps over the otter wall to canter away down the road to the mainland. Presumably it had jumped the wall to get onto the island, or swam across. But why?

Walking down to the lighthouse in the last of the daylight. A toad lying in the path. I squat and place the back of my hand on the toad's skin. It is cold, the toad sluggish. It sits there on the path, looking straight ahead, doing nothing much. I can't understand how it came to be there. Before the bridge builders had come with their heavy machinery, blasting and infilling and laying rock armour, there had been patches of bog on the island, now there were almost none. Toads migrate back to the water pools where they were spawned to spawn again in their turn. Had the toad swum across from the mainland? Most unlikely. Crawled along the road, over the bridge and under the gate? Feasible, perhaps. Had a predator – a kestrel, say – dropped the toad from on high while flying over the island? More likely, but would birds of prey take a foul-tasting, poison-skinned toad? I left the toad where it was and continued my slow perambulation around the island. In the morning the toad was gone. I never came across another.

That second summer voles were everywhere on the island. The previous summer there'd been very few. Voles reproduce so fast that every third year there's a population explosion and then they get decimated by predators. Boom and bust. I came across the voles all the time on my rounds that summer, leisurely munching blades of grass. As I crept politely by they would look up at me, munching away, with an 'Ooh, don't you mind me, young man, you just carry on' look on their faces.

Then one morning I got up to find the path between the cottage and the hide littered with the corpses of partially eaten voles. I had my suspicions as to the culprit of this mass slaughter, for I'd caught glimpses of lithe musteline creatures running across the paths, but these sightings were so fleeting I was never sure if it was otter, pine marten or mink I was seeing, or just shadows caused by tired eyes. The morning of the massacre, a guest staying in the cottage told me she had spotted 'a huge red cat' on the island the previous evening. If mink and pine marten and roe deer (and toads) were using the bridge to move between the mainland and Skye, and exploring the island en route, why not Scottish wildcats? Or foxes?

The next morning I came across more mauled corpses. The idea of a wildcat living on the island was flattering (they're extremely elusive and shy), but a trip into Kyle and a 'LOST' notice in the window of the supermarket revealed the nature of the beast.

I telephoned a young woman in the village, who squealed with joy before bursting into tears. She arrived swiftly at the gate of the island clutching a large wickerwork cage and the arm of her sister. I left them alone to wander the island and withdrew to my room with a book. After an hour or so there was a knock on the door. The woman stood clutching the cage. I bend down to peer inside. A very fat ginger tomcat yowled and hissed, raised a claw and spat at me. The young woman remained tearful.

'It must have been just so terrible for him,' she mewed, 'lost in all those brambles and alone in the freezing cold without any food or milk.'

I told her about the slaughtered voles. 'I'll bet he had a wonderful time,' I said. 'And he definitely ate well.'

'But he's so miserable. Look!' she sobbed, holding the cage on high. The spitting psychopath snarled and clawed at the bars of his cage. 'Just you let me get out of here so I can rip your head off,' was the look on *his* face.

That afternoon a short, olive-skinned man in his mid-fifties, immaculately dressed, almost regimental in his bearing, stood waiting at the gate for a tour. There was only him that day.

'Come to look at the lighthouse,' he said.

We meandered down the path past the bothy to the Long Room and I began my talk on the history of the island and the Trust and Maxwell. After a few minutes I could see the man was getting impatient.

'Are we going to see the lighthouse next?' he said. I locked up and took him down the cobbled path to the lighthouse, and shortly we were standing out on the balcony, gazing over the island and the sea. The man looked relaxed now. He breathed in deeply, sighed, straightened up.

'The tower and gangway are in a bit of a sorry state, I know,' I said. 'The big hope for us is the National Lottery Heritage Fund. We've applied to them and other charities for funding and if we get it we can renovate the lighthouse. We should be hearing back from them soon.' And if the applications were turned down, I knew, we wouldn't be able to renovate the lighthouse and the Trust would continue to struggle for its survival.

And I had been taking stock of my own situation. My savings were running low and I'd no money coming in. I'd been living on a shoestring for years and I was getting fed up with always being broke, dodging around, everything being second hand; of buying richer people's cast-offs, picking up what others dropped. I was sliding towards my forties and still hadn't any of the trappings expected of a successful modern man. Where were the wife and kids, the house and garden, the career path and a snug, steady income? All these had passed me by, while friends of my own age were now deep into familydom, safe within the walls of their chosen career, drawing a salary that increased incrementally year on year. They had pension plans; I owned a pallet-load of books in a barn somewhere down south and that was about it. Old friends and I were drifting apart, and whenever we spoke on the telephone a noticeable gulf had opened up between us.

'I used to be a lighthouse keeper, you know,' the man said. 'On the Gower in Wales at the end. But I moved around too. All over, I went. Loved it, I did.'

The man leant back against the railings. 'It was a good life, lighthouse keeping, and they looked after you. Job for life, I thought.'

We climbed back down the lighthouse stairs and stood yakking on the gangway under a light drizzle. I asked the man where he worked now, now that there were no more lighthouse keepers left.

'Work in a dog-food factory just outside Swansea, I do,' he said, 'Hate it, I do.'

We walked on round the island in the rain.

≈

Workcrew Wednesdays went and came. The day I'm remembering, Marcus was away over the other side of the island flame-gunning the paths. John the chairman was hacking at the brambles with his long-handled scythe. I had a tour of one – a handsome grey-haired woman in a blue and white polka-dot dress. She wore large, gold hoop earrings and was one of those rare people who possess a butterfly mind, and it had been a long tour because we had found so much to talk about. We were leaning against the lighthouse wall in the mid-afternoon sun, enjoying the warmth of the day and the meeting of minds, looking across to Kyleakin Beach, discussing the Trust, the island, life, and Maxwell. I'd been rereading Botting's biography.

'In the end,' I said, 'you could make a case that he chose to live in such inaccessible places because of his sexuality. Remote, difficult to get to, away from prying eyes. He could bring whomever he liked up here and no one could see what was going on. And all those winters in Morocco . . . He wouldn't have been the first or the last to go there looking for young men. Don't you think Maxwell's homosexuality provoked the way he lived his life?'

In these modern times we tend to forget that up until 1967 homosexuality was illegal in England and Wales, and remained illegal in Scotland until 1980. A homosexual stayed in the closet to stay out of gaol and out of the press. There's a passage in Richard Frere's book about an evening in the lighthouse cottage. Frere had gone across to the island on company business and while there witnessed Maxwell raging at Andrew Scot, upbraiding him for misdemeanours both real and imagined. Scot was sent to his room. Cutting the uneasy silence that followed, Maxwell said to Frere: 'Can you not understand? That boy will destroy me.' When I had first read that, I'd thought Maxwell must have been raving, deluded, paranoid. He was unhappy and isolated. The Sandaig fire had recently destroyed almost everything he owned and, although he didn't know it, he was critically ill and only months away from the grave. Almost the only thing he had left was his reputation.

Maxwell wasn't keen on Andrew Scot making friends in the villages or spending too long away from the island. Because he was terrified Scot might go gossiping and let the cat out of the bag? Scot would have seen and heard a lot, been privy to some of Maxwell's secrets while living with him. It is no wonder that Maxwell became paranoid after relations broke down between Scot and him.

'Perhaps it was well known up here anyway,' the woman said, 'Maxwell's sexuality.'

'Do you think so?'

The woman thought for a moment. 'I think too much emphasis is placed on a person's sexual persuasion these days. Why should it matter what anyone "is"? Also, it was a very different world forty years ago. When I was a young woman, if a man kissed me I thought it was because he liked me, I didn't know it meant he wanted to go to bed with me. We were much more innocent back then.'

Sometimes, on tours, I'd stand with a group of visitors in the Long Room in front of the photographs of Maxwell, chatting about his life, and someone would pipe up, 'So he never married then?' and someone else might smirk and there'd be whispers.

'Homosexuality was as common then as it is today,' the

polka-dot butterfly woman said. 'It's always been there. Criminalizing something just sends it underground. A lot of homosexuals sublimated their urges in those days – shut themselves away in the priesthood or became school-masters or dons.'

'And look what's come bubbling up to the surface as a result of that,' I said.

The woman grimaced. 'So much, then, for trying to run away from what you are. As for whether he was the other thing . . .'

'It lingers around him, *boys.*'

'Not everyone acts on their urges or, for that matter, their inclinations. I don't know whether Gavin Maxwell wanted to corrupt young boys or not. I know there's always been the whispering, but if he had been a paedophile I think there would have been accusations of impropriety or sexual abuse by now. The rest, unless someone comes forward, is speculation and innuendo.'

Perhaps Maxwell just liked having teenagers around him, much as a certain kind of heterosexual male will be more likely to employ a pretty young woman over one who is losing her looks and has a more jaded view of the world and of him. Maxwell always remained a bit of an adolescent himself, part of him always stuck at sixteen. And teenagers are cheaper to employ, and more biddable than adults.

Maxwell was also involved with Braehead Secondary School in Fife. The coeducational school's progressive headmaster, R. F. Mackenzie, was a firm believer in and proselytizer for the importance of outdoor pursuits (mountain climbing, sailing, etc.), as opposed to organized competitive sports, as part of a rounded education. Maxwell supported Mackenzie's theories and wrote in his introduction to Mackenzie's *Escape from the Classroom*:

> [R. F. Mackenzie] believes that intimate contact with the countryside, as part of a term's curriculum, can build and sustain a child's personality despite parental and other disorders of background.
>
> . . . In nature a child senses an order and security often lacking in his home surroundings, and thus becomes part of a unity elusive in urban upbringing.

In the early 60s Maxwell had groups of Braehead schoolchildren and their teachers down at Sandaig exploring the sea and hills around. Maxwell's schooldays had been unhappy and he hadn't much belief in traditional teaching systems. He was interested in people and he was interested in pedagogy and comparative psychology.

For many years Maxwell supported financially Ahmed ben Lahsen Tija, a young Moroccan he had employed as a guide, translator and companion during his winters in Morocco, and who had helped him research and illustrate

Lords of the Atlas. For over a decade, Maxwell also sponsored a Sicilian who, in the 1950s, had helped him with research for *God Protect Me from My Friends* and *The Ten Pains of Death.* (Maxwell put this man – who referred to him in his letters as *padrino* 'godfather' – through medical school and only discontinued support in 1966, when he was staving off bankruptcy.) Does there necessarily need to have been something sinister behind Maxwell's association with teenagers?

Jimmy Watt was fifteen and about to leave school when Maxwell interviewed him in 1958. Jimmy remained in Maxwell's employ until he was twenty-two years old. He remained close until Maxwell's death, and spoke of him as a father figure. Terry Nutkins's story is stranger. He went to live at Sandaig full-time in the Easter of 1961, as a thirteen-year-old. Maxwell became his legal guardian, with the consent of Terry's parents, and gave written assurance that he would provide the boy with three hours of schooling a day. These days such an arrangement almost certainly would not be allowed. As my polka-dot friend said, we were much more innocent back then.

When I was fifteen and first read Maxwell's Camus-feàrna books I saw nothing odd about a middle-aged man living with a couple of teenage boys, otters and dogs in a place that was a cross between an Outward Bound centre and a zoo. In fact it seemed perfect and I wished I could have been part of it, living with them. What a wonderful world for a teenage boy, I thought. Only now does it strike me how strange it was for a man (whatever his sexual preference) to employ young teenagers to go and live and work for him in a house miles away from others. It seems bizarre now, and highly suspect to a mind that has lost its innocence residing in much more suspicious, amoral and knowing times. I have never come across a similar setup. A fog of uncertainty can only be dispelled by facts. Whether in reality there was anything untoward going on only the otter boys know for sure, and the men they are now haven't mentioned anything. I would have thought that if either of these men associated Sandaig with dreadful events during their boyhood they'd have wanted to get as far away from the place and its associations as possible. Yet once they left Sandaig, after making lives elsewhere, when they were in a position financially to do so, they returned. Today, Jimmy Watt lives within sight of Sandaig, and Terry Nutkins, until his death from leukaemia in September 2012, lived with his brood only a mile or two away from that place.

≈

On 26 July, surrounded by a royal-blue sea lit by a bright orange sun in a royal-blue sky, Pete and I were idling in a warm breeze gossiping. We were standing side by side in front of the cottage, each partly listening to the bletherings of the other, but mostly taking in the goings-on in the villages across the water and scanning for boats, otters, dolphins and interesting birds. Pete was deep into a bafflingly tedious explanation as to why he'd not be able to take his next tour and could I do it for him, when the pretty *Hebridean Princess* cruise ship swept out of the Kylerhea Narrows and steamed towards Kyle of Lochalsh. In itself, this was not so noteworthy an occurrence – the ship was a regular visitor to these waters. But when a hulking battleship-grey gunboat and a swarm of police launches hove into view Pete and I were forced to stop wittering and get a hold on the situation.

'Binoculars,' Pete ordered.

I fetched binoculars.

'Didn't I hear somewhere the Queen was hiring the *Hebridean Princess* to cruise around the Western Isles like she did in the old days?' Pete said.

'Before they got rid of the Royal Yacht?' I said. 'I've seen it on the quayside in Edinburgh, going nowhere.'

'They're mooring up in Kyle.'

'The gunboat isn't.'

The gunboat steamed towards us. I studied it through the binoculars.

'HMS *Argyll*,' I read. 'I can see civilians wandering about on deck and . . . men with guns.'

Four police launches bobbed around at a not-so-discreet distance from the *Hebridean Princess*. The cruise ship tied up and lowered a gangway onto Kyle quay. I noticed that a couple of brown shipping containers had been placed in such a way as to shield from view the gangway as it stretched from ship to shore.

I turned the binoculars on the gunboat as it powered towards the island and sped by, pushing a foamy sea out in front of it. The men with guns – soldiers with fingers on the triggers of high-velocity rifles, strutting up and down the decks – made it all seem less of a lark, less of a jolly summer jaunt. A man in a uniform with peaked cap trained his binoculars on me. I raised an arm and waved. No one on the ship waved back.

Pete snorted. 'The royals've probably stopped for afternoon tea or something in Kyle. So, can you do Thursday for me?'

Pete sloped off to his car and to the sound of crashing gears and painfully high revs bullied it back over the bridge. I locked up and walked into Kyle.

'The usual?' the barmaid said as I stepped in.

'Please.'

'Did you see? They're here waiting on Prince Charles and Camilla driving down from somewhere.'

Sitting with your drink on the sofas in the bar of the Lochalsh Hotel you can look over to Kyle Harbour and the train station and across to Kyleakin and Skye. I lounged and awaited the arrival of the Heir Apparent and his wife.

'They've been asking at the harbourmaster's for fresh langoustine and lobster,' the barmaid whispered on one of my return visits to the bar.

I drifted back to the island and sat on the bench outside the cottage beneath a dying afternoon sun and waited, binoculars at the ready. The bridge cast its afternoon shadow over the cottage. A fleet of immaculate Range Rovers swept in tight formation onto Kyle Quay and disappeared behind the brown shipping containers. Almost immediately the *Hebridean Princess* slipped her moorings and headed towards the island. The police launches buzzed busily around the mother ship. As the *Hebridean Princess* passed the island I scrutinized the decks but there was no one to be seen. A policeman on one of the launches stood at a railing and seemed to want a game of who can stare longest. I didn't bother waving. I lowered my binoculars. Up on the bridge, police cars with their blue lights flashing milled around, presumably to prevent rogue Native children lobbing stones.

I jogged across to the west side of the island. It was late now, the sun falling into the sea. A grey mist lurked all along the shoreline of Raasay, ten miles away, and I could make out the bulk of the gunboat, its grey hull fading in and out, almost invisible in the murky haze. I clambered over rocks and plonked down on a handkerchief-sized patch of grass beside the crunched-up remains of a crab. The royals sailed away to the north-west, into the sunset, heading for the Outer Hebrides. The police outriders attended them. The grey protector edged out of the mist and joined the convoy. I, on my rocky islet, sat on until I grew cold, with only the night and an uncertain future to sail into.

≈

The following day, a Workcrew Wednesday, Marcus and I spent the day with pickaxes and crowbars hauling out boulders to plant saplings. Only a very thin layer of sphagnum moss and peat covers the bedrock of the island. When Marcus left as usual at 4.40 p.m. I set about making a woodpile under the bridge and scattering dead bracken and brambles over it. I was resting from my labours, and remembering a visitor telling me that for him the West Highlands were 'a preview of heaven', when a man of medium height with short grey hair came walking up the path. As he came closer I spotted an embroidered Highlands and Islands Council logo on the blue fleece he was wearing. My first thought was that someone had observed me piling up logs under the bridge and instead of appreciating the fine habitat I was creating for pine martens and other interesting creatures, had phoned the council to report a pyromaniac.

'Hello,' the man said.

'Hello,' I said.

There was a pause. I wasn't sure whether this was a 'trespasser' situation or the, albeit stilted, beginning of a stern reprimand I probably deserved for stacking highly combustible materials under a public right of way.

Then the man said: 'I'm Donald Mitchell. I—'

'Oh!' I said and a knot tightened in my stomach because I knew exactly who he was.

I'd only ever seen photographs of him: battling with the wheel of a boat in a gale in 1969; sitting at a table in the sun outside the lighthouse cottage with John Lister-Kaye and Jimmy Watt and a scramble of dogs. Young. They were all young then. If Donald Mitchell was seventeen in those photos, he would have been in his mid-fifties that afternoon he jumped over the wall and strolled up to me. In *The White Island*, Lister-Kaye's book, Donald will always be seventeen, even when we have all passed away.

We stood silently for a time. There was so much I wanted to ask him, the last otter boy. He had the bluest of blue eyes.

'We used to cut turf from the hill behind the house up there,' he eventually said, and pointed: 'For the fires. We flew a flag from a pole by the water tank.'

'Have you been back to the island before?' I asked.

'Once or twice. Virginia McKenna contacted me once, to see if I had anything I could donate for the Long Room.'

I left the woodpile and we walked along the path towards the house. I wanted to show him what we'd been doing.

'You've good paths now,' he said. 'When I lived here most of the island was just rough. We had a ram and a couple of goats. They'd eat anything. And we burnt off the heather in the summer, to keep it manageable.' He stopped. 'This . . . this must be where the generator shed was, somewhere here.'

'It was demolished during the renovations,' I said. 'I don't know why.'

'One of my jobs was to shut down the generator last thing at night. I always took Gavin's deerhounds with me to give them a run. But really . . . it was because I was scared.'

I could see memories clouding his eyes. 'There weren't any streetlights in Kyleakin back then and once I shut down the generator there'd be dead silence and pitch black. When there was a moon it wasn't too bad but I was only young.'

We walked on and stopped beside Teko's memorial, looking down the loch.

Tell me all about Gavin, I thought, *and Jimmy and Richard Frere.*

'A cup of tea?' I said. 'Coffee? Something stronger?'

Donald shook his head. 'I should be going soon. It's a long drive north. I was over on Skye and thought I'd look in, but . . .' He seemed to shrink into himself a little.

'There was an advertisement. In the *Press and Journal*. I had relatives on Skye. They saw the ad and told me about it and I wrote but heard nothing for a month or so. Then Richard Frere telephoned and invited me to go and stay at his house in Drumnadrochit for a few days. So he could check me out, I suppose, see if I'd make a suitable companion for Gavin here on the island.

'Gavin was already ill by then and wasn't around much. It was mostly me and John Lister-Kaye, working on the aviaries and fencing and looking after the animals they'd collected for the zoo. Once, when Gavin was here, he sent me to fetch the doctor and I got mixed up and went over in the dinghy to Kyleakin instead of Kyle. I telephoned him from the phone box in Kyleakin to say I couldn't find a surgery anywhere in the village and he blew up at me. He had a quick temper. But he was in quite a lot of pain all the time those last months.'

Afternoon light was fading into dusk. *Please talk on*, I thought.

'Is there anything you'd like to ask me before I go?'

Everything would have been the true answer. *Tell me about the old days.*

'Do you pronounce it 'Teeko' or 'Téko',' I said.

'It rhymes with echo.'

Donald gazed down the loch. 'Gavin wrote me a letter from his hospital bed in Inverness a few days before he died. I gave a copy of it to Virginia.'

'We have it,' I said. 'It's in the Long Room.'

The letter, sent to Donald at the end of August 1969, consists of a long humorous poem about rabbits and their reproductive habits. Douglas Botting included that part of the letter in his biography. Maxwell's postscript, however, wasn't included:

P.S. Having got that important collection of observations off my chest, I'll tell you what else is off my chest. Three litres of fluid were drained off my right lung last night. That is the effect of straight pleurisy, which is possibly unconnected with the serious trouble, and has been responsible for my feeling so unutterably lousy. Too lousy to tell you how much your work has been appreciated; and the pleasant atmosphere you bring with you. I think we have the makings of a happy family at Kyleakin, though since your arrival I haven't been able to contribute much to it myself.

Yrs, GM

P.P.S. I hope you'll spend a bit of time with the crow, as Davy did.

'I took the crow with me when I left,' Donald said as he opened the door of his car. 'Why is it that the wild creatures we keep as pets always come to a premature and sticky end?'

I waved as he drove away. Meeting Donald was how I imagined it would be to meet one of the real-life children Arthur Ransome conjured into characters for his *Swallows and Amazons* books. Ransome's books, like Maxwell's, had captivated me as a boy. Reading them I'd wished I could somehow step into the stories, close the covers and fall away into the world of adventures they described. We are all frustratingly earthbound, destined to wade through the banalities of reality; brilliants trapped in the cotton wool of circumstance.

Seven

The Fall

Ever since reading Maxwell's first book, *Harpoon at a Venture*, I had wanted to visit Soay – the small island beyond the Isle of Skye that Maxwell had owned for a few years in the mid-1940s. Maxwell had used Soay harbour as a base for his shark-fishing boats, and a disused storehouse above the harbour was converted to a processing plant where the islanders cut up the sharks and rendered down the livers to extract the precious oil. It was an altogether vile business and not something the islanders were overly keen to help with. Maxwell poured money (his own and other people's) into the venture but after only three seasons the company was put into liquidation, the island was put into receivership, Maxwell retreated south and eventually the islanders, like others of the smaller Hebridean islands, petitioned the government for evacuation.

The previous winter I had driven over to Skye and to Elgol and taken the impossibly steep road that winds down through the village to the slipway, where I parked and sat in the car looking over the sea to Soay.

Elgol, lying only two and a half miles across Loch Scavaig from Soay, is the village where an Englishwoman, Lillian Comber, went to live during World War II. Under the nom de plume 'Lillian Beckwith', she wrote a string of semi-autobiographical 'comic' novels about life in and around Elgol, the first of which was *The Hills is Lonely*.

Off-white clouds scudded across a pale blue sky. A fierce blustery wind batted gulls around the sky, making them appear drunken and disorientated. Gannets circled and dived into the frothing tossing sea, reminding me of Stuka bombers zeroing in on targets in all those World War II movies I'd watched as a boy. The car shook and rocked. Spray flew from the crests of tightly packed waves over the rocks and onto the road and the windscreen of my car.

I forced the door open, stepped out into the wind and a gust blew my hat far up a hill out of reach. The wind buffeted me this way and that as I bent into it and battled my way to the lee of the slipway wall, where stacks of creels, coils of rope and floats and plastic fish boxes had been stashed safe from the prevailing wind. Waves were smashing shoreward onto the slipway and spume – froth and foam like sheep's fleece – came rolling up the slope towards me. I squatted low and looked out to sea towards Soay, where I could make out houses dotted along a road above a bay.

The figure-of-eight-shaped Soay, as an outlying island, has always lacked both a ferry service and public utility services such as electricity, telephone, piped water and sewerage. A livelihood was always fragile here. In June 1953 the SS *Hebrides* called at Soay, loaded the thirty or so islanders and their possessions aboard and took them south to the larger island of Mull, where they were given crofts and were able to find work. Only Tex Geddes, Maxwell's friend from his SOE instructor days and the chief harpooner during the shark-fishing venture, remained on the island with his wife Jan. Tex, something of a local legend (he once threatened to eat the German laird of the nearby island of Eigg), bought the island from the receivers, became 'Laird of Soay' and until his death in 1998 wrested a living by fishing and breeding ponies. He wrote a book, *Hebridean Sharker*, about his time with Maxwell and after, drank hard, told stories and warned off 'trespassers' to his island with an infamous, ferocious rudeness. Or so some say.

Tex is dead, another of the old Highland buccaneers who 'lived it', gone to his grave. Soay now is like many of the other small islands of the Hebrides – the Crowlins, Scarp, Mingulay, Noss, St Kilda. Where families once lived, laughed and grumbled; where children played; where there were once schools, working crofts, whisky and stories and envy and lust, there are now a few holiday homes and a smattering of part-time summer residents.

The majority of these smaller islands, though, remain abandoned. Quiet, moribund; gone back to nature.

I hadn't got to Soay that storm-tossed day. Only a few miles away across that raging sea, it was as unreachable as the moon. But that second summer, one fine day in August, Sandy and I tied a couple of borrowed kayaks onto the roof of his van and drove over the hills to Glenbrittle.

We paddled for what seemed like hours. We struck out for a distant headland, rounded it and paddled along under dripping fern-covered cliffs until we spotted the entrance to Soay harbour two miles away across open sea. We rested, drank and, refreshed, paddled on. The sea away from the coast was flat, dark blue, profound and sparkling; it blinded me with reflected sunlight. Kayaking in the main requires only brute force; arms and upper body propel the kayak forward. We powered on.

A sand bar at the entrance to Soay harbour was a con-tributing factor to the failure of Maxwell's shark-fishing venture. His boats had to wait for the tide to be right before they could set out to hunt or deliver the carcasses to the factory. Business held up by nature. Sandy and I reached the bar just before low water and our kayaks grounded. The harbour was emptying out over the shells and sand. I followed Sandy as he shuffled and levered his way up and over the bar into the deeper water of the harbour. Above us a ram, motionless, stood sentinel on an outcrop of rock in the sun, watching us.

A small yacht flying a Dutch flag was anchored in the wide, sheltered expanse of the harbour. As we paddled past, two blubbery women in swimsuits, sitting in the cockpit drinking from cans of beer, waved lazily and disinterestedly. There was a square stone building with half its roof missing and a collection of entirely roofless post-World War II prefabs on the rocks above the harbour. We beached the kayaks in a dried-out cove and clambered over rocks to the buildings – Maxwell's processing plant. What looked like the front end of a steam train, all inch-thick curved slabs of cast iron, rivets and rust – decades of rust – stood near massive galvanized tanks. Most of the prefabs were empty, their concrete floors cracked and decaying. One of them was stuffed with partially deflated, mouldering fishing buoys, crushed lobster pots, broken creels, scarred and scuffed plastic fish boxes, empty pots of paint and tools made useless by rust – a jumble of forgotten objects, left out for too long in the rain.

On the opposite shore a couple of wooden work-boats lay in the mud, their hulls splayed open like dried-up carcasses in the veldt. The whole site was a graveyard of long-forgotten items.

'Some of this stuff could be useful,' Sandy said. 'I may have to borrow a RIB and come back and have a proper root around.'

For Sandy this place spelt opportunity, more stuff to hoard away 'just in case'. But for me the sense of abandonment, of the end of dreams, was all-pervasive and total and depressing. I'd seen photographs of the site in books and magazine articles – men at work with long-handled flensing knives slicing up basking sharks; the heads of these mammoth fish being craned over the rocks to be dumped into the harbour; the area behind the buildings a boneyard strewn with discarded basking-shark cartilage. Not particularly pleasant photos to look at, true enough, but they were full of visceral life and death. Now there was just an end-of-days feeling here.

We sat on a patch of grass in the sun and ate sandwiches, the silence broken occasionally by a peal of girlish laughter from the Dutch yacht, by an oystercatcher trilling as it shot across the still green water below us. We hacked our way through brambles and head-high bracken to the other side of the island to take a look at the houses along the bay, but there was no movement there. The few houses that weren't derelict were empty of signs of life or love – faded window frames and peeling wallpaper, closed and shuttered doors, dark interiors and silence.

Sandy was less loquacious than usual that day on Soay. 'Sad,' was all he said about the abandoned, *Mary Celeste* village. And he didn't go poking about among the remains.

We picked our way back to the cove. The tide was rising

and the sea had begun to lap at the kayaks, lifting and dropping them gently with every ripple it sent to bounce off the rocks. The Dutch yacht was quiescent. Soay's ghosts slumbered on. Under light spotting rain we climbed into the kayaks and paddled away over the sand bar and back to Skye, where clouds coalesced and spilled over the Cuillins like foam.

≈

Towards the end of August, above our small acreage, rainbows arrived. Double and triple rainbows were common. I'd be chopping or digging or weeding on a day of sunshine and showers and catch a cold wind on my face and look up to see a ball of dense purple cloud coming up the loch fast. I'd duck into the lobby of the house or the bothy to watch the oncoming spew of rain drench the island, listen to hailstones clattering against window panes, pattering on the grass in front of me. The storm cloud would speed on westwards to leave silence for a moment before the gusting wind returned. The sun would come out again and I'd see the rainbow – its brilliant spectrum of colours against the cerulean blue of the sky, its ends planted either side of the island in the indigo blue of the sea, a lone angel-white herring gull flying under the arch and away.

These squalls brought with them a quality of light that I have only ever experienced in India during the dying weeks of the monsoon, when the atmosphere has been rinsed of dust and pollen and airborne pollution and all that is left is clean, crisp air. On days such as these on the island I had a clear view across the Inner Sound to the Old Man of Storr on the north-eastern tip of Skye and to the Isle of Rona, twenty miles and more beyond.

On other, more autumnal days, the sun would shine milky, hidden by great wet slops of dawdling grey stratus cloud. A crack in this murk would appear and a fan of sunlight would shoot out to set a patch of sea aflame – angels' torches, we call them, God's rays come down from the heavens.

≈

I had come to look forward to Pete's visits after he'd taken a tour – the slam of the bothy door and the slap-slip of his wellington boots as he slobbed his way down the steps to my door. His visits were fleeting, he was always in a rush to be off, so I knew something was up when he knocked on the door and for once accepted my offer of a cup of tea and a seat to sit down in.

'I've decided to quit as a trustee.' Pete was never one to beat about the bush. 'And I won't be taking the tours any more.' He wasn't as well as he had been. Pete was of an age when the body starts paying one back for all the assaults launched against it during the early indulgent years. He had decided to let some of his responsibilities go. The trust was one of those.

'And the tours cut into my day,' he said. 'In the morning I'm hanging around waiting to see if I have one, and after taking a tour I'm drained and just want to go home and sleep.'

'I know what you mean,' I said. But I was sad he was leaving, and told him so.

'You're just sad because you'll have to take all the tours from now on.'

But it wasn't like that. For all his bluff and bluster, Pete cared – about the island, about the villages and the villagers, about the community as a whole. And he meddled where many believed an Incomer had no place meddling because he wanted to help, and be of use.

Pete left and I walked around the island several times. The foxgloves, of which there were many on the island that summer, were fading, their purple trumpets dropping silently and unseen to the floor. Blackberries were on their way. I sat for a long time on the grass in front of the hide looking west to the isles in the Inner Sound. As the sun fell towards the hills of Raasay, I watched five gannets flying like ace fighter pilots over the Inner Sound, adjusting flight path and angle of descent as they wheeled high through the blue before checking in flight to fold their wings and dive, a splash of white, into the sea. They surfaced, flapping their wings like mad to clamber heavily back into the air, pick up speed, adjust angles of attack, then dive on folded wings into the blue once more. Ever since seeing those gannets taking such delight in the gale that day at Elgol, for me, they have become harbingers of bad weather.

I walked down to the lighthouse and stood in the wind on the gappy planking of the gangway. The tide was in. Lighthouse Bay was full of sea. Wavelets journeyed by beneath me. There was a crowd of people out in Kyleakin, strolling along the beach and laughing; kids playing football on the green. It was one of those restless evenings when the villagers, reluctant to go indoors, roved about until well after dusk. The summer solstice was a distant memory. The days were getting shorter.

Two weeks later, two weeks into September, during a conversation with one of the trustees, I heard the words I would have seen coming if my dreaming head hadn't been elsewhere that summer.

'We were turned down for funding by all the organizations we applied to. It was felt our needs are not as great as some of the other applicants. I'm not sure where that leaves you.'

I'd become as emotionally involved with the island as with a lover. When I was away from it I thought about it. I felt a responsibility to it, and I thought I had found home. But the island could never be home, not truly. I was a caretaker, a seasonal curator, nothing more. And I had stripped the newness from the island; there were no more secrets.

I didn't know where I'd go, but that afternoon, with

those few words uttered by the trustee, I felt sure that my time on the island had come to an end. I would miss it.

The weather worsened and the solemn hills were in silhouette by 7.30 p.m. The tours dropped off to virtually nil. The vegetation slowed up and shrank back into itself, into the earth and the rocks. The bird life on the island went through the change. The trilling curlew came once again to prod the shoreline at low tide and the eider ducks bobbed and *oohed* in the Inner Sound.

In the same week of October as the previous year, I heard the *ssiiii* of flocks of redwing rushing over the island in the dark. The strange little marriage of mergansers – absent since late spring – returned to feed around the shoreline, only the lucky drake had now increased his harem to three. The honeysuckle was still in flower, the dandelions still showed their leonine heads, buttercups still brightened the cobbled path. Blackberries ripened, shrivelled. The screeching terns had long since departed; sightings of razorbills, guillemots and puffins became increasingly rare. The seals were making moves, leaving for their pupping grounds. Montbretia flowers withered, then fell.

One low tide I spotted what I at first took to be an otter cub, down among the steep barnacle-encrusted rocks in front of the house. I stalked closer and from a vantage point on the rocks above, peered down at the creature. It munched a small dogfish, chomping and stopping every now and then to sniff and look around before chomping on. It was a mink. I was ten feet above it. It couldn't catch my scent, but somehow it knew. It looked up, saw me, dropped the fish and set off along the rocks towards the old jetty. I followed. The mink stopped and glared at me, outrage all over its face. It held its ground, peevish, daring me to follow. Then it turned and trotted on to disappear into the rocks by the alder tree.

I found a drowned shrew in the plastic rainfall gauge that I kept by the lighthouse shed, and came across a field mouse floating lifeless in a bucket of water I'd left by the bothy.

Walking back to the island in the rain one afternoon after a visit to the Lochalsh Hotel bar I found a mouse curled up and cold on the wet concrete threshold of the door to my room.

On 18 October, a day of fine drizzle, I stood by the hide and counted fifty-five geese flying south. The following day I watched a hundred or more pass high over the island, jink, and head south-east down Loch Alsh. That same day, while sitting up in the bothy with the door open, I heard the unmistakable honking of swans, and rushed out. There were more of them than I could count, flying high, high overhead, in a perfect V, heading down the loch.

By the end of October the bracken on the island was long dead and the rosebay willowherb had reduced to desiccated stalks. The gorse was beginning to flower again, and gale-strewn leaves and rowan berries littered the island paths. By the end of November – the month of the dead – along with the last of the tourists, the house guests, the flowers and the summer, I was gone.

≈

Virginia McKenna had sent money. The trustees bought a sundial to commemorate Johnny 'Ach' Macrae's vision and vitality. A local man had engraved a brass plaque to decorate the dial. Johnny's son-in-law came across to the island and cut a footing for the pedestal from a prominent rock on the lawn in front of the house. For a week, with Duncan wielding a stone-cutter and slopping around buckets of cement, it was like old times – shouts and machinery, lights blazing, doors open, celebratory drams drunk at the end of a day's work.

John the chairman borrowed a Clan Macrae tartan rug for the unveiling on that mid-October day of wind and rain. Cakes and drinks were prepared in the cottage kitchen and I lit a fire in the Long Room. The trustees arrived, and some of their spouses. Johnny Ach's widow and daughters came, and the new harbourmaster. Duncan trundled Johnny's grandchild down the path in a pushchair.

And Jimmy Watt came, swaddled in wet-weather gear. A shock of white hair and a shy geniality. Now in his sixties, he stood in rumpled socks on the rug in the room where as a young man with his whole working life before him he'd stood once before. I'd wanted to meet him for years, to sit by a fire with a dram and listen to him reminisce about Maxwell and life down at Sandaig and the old days. But for people like him, the familiars of the famous – the Christopher Robins of this world – apart from those who like to bask in reflected glory, I think there must always be a *But what about me?* Everyone wants to know about the celebrity friend, or the immortalized family member, but not much about the familiar, who is merely the possessor of memories, a brain to be picked. And so I'd fought shy of bothering Jimmy Watt. And I liked to believe that my interest in Gavin Maxwell was that of a scholar and not that of a fan. I'd met enough 'Maxwell nuts' on the tours to divine a distinction between the fanatically obsessed and other visitors who had been moved or enchanted by the Camusfeàrna books and had come to the island out of curiosity. Some very strange people came to the island, lingering in the Long Room and sighing and telling me how much they wished they could have met Gavin Maxwell. I didn't want to believe I was like these fans, but I probably was.

The invited that day assembled in the warmth of the Long Room driftwood fire. I sat on Maxwell's sofa beside the fireplace, clutching a beaker of red wine, observing everyone and thinking: *This is how it should be – a roomful of people and talk.*

A trustee came and sat beside me. I liked and admired her. She was one of the old buccaneers. She had come to the West Highlands from England in the 1950s as a young woman with a head filled with the same romantic notions as us all. She had met Maxwell, had known Tex Geddes and had worked on boats with some of the crew from Maxwell's shark-fishing venture. And she was a friend of Jimmy Watt's.

'Everyone says what a wonderful difference you've made to the island,' she said, tapping her beaker against mine.

'I don't think I can stay on,' I said. 'I can't afford to remain as I am, and if I find work elsewhere I'll have to leave because I won't be free to take the tours or work on the island. It's impossible.'

'I don't think that would necessarily be the case,' the trustee said. Over the years her English accent had mingled with the melodic tones of the Highlander. 'The tours are almost finished for the year now and there's little to do on the island over the winter. You'd have the time to earn enough somewhere to see you through next year. There's always more than one way of looking at these things. If you really want to do something, as you know well yourself, you can always find a way.'

After an hour, after cakes and drinks and talk, John the chairman ushered us out onto the lawn where the Clan Macrae tartan was draped over the sundial. A strong south-westerly flung rain into our faces, drenching us. The streets of the two villages were deserted – everyone gone indoors. John shouted a few words over the bellowing wind in praise of Johnny Ach and removed the rug. We clapped. Someone took a photograph of Johnny Ach's family standing behind the sundial in front of a backdrop of grey sky and green sea. Then we trooped back into the Long Room to stand in the warm and dry off and sign a card thanking Virginia McKenna for her cheque. People gathered up their things, got ready to go home.

As the others were heading out into the rain, a trustee standing beside Jimmy Watt called me over.

Jimmy and I spoke for a few moments, mumbling something or other about lightships and boats. He remembered I'd returned a document marked 'Private and Confidential' to him some months previously. He'd been busy, he said, and apologized for not thanking me before. Then we shook hands and he went away out into the wind and the rain. He has the hands of a sailor, or a builder – big, battered, capable hands.

That evening, as I was finishing tidying up the Long Room, I looked down the room to check everything was okay and caught sight of Raef Payne's portrait of his friend hanging above the fireplace and a wave of sadness crashed through me.

This is all that is left: moth-eaten carpets, antique furniture riddled with woodworm, a handful of mementoes

– a museum housing the decaying effects of a long-dead man, a fire long gone cold.

This is all that is ever left. You're born, you blaze, you die. I didn't even believe I belonged in the Highlands.

There were some jobs going with the Highland Council (water-quality tester, mobile-library van driver, a couple of others). I filled out application forms and posted them off, but I had more than a hunch that the employment gaps in my CV, along with my Incomer status and an appalling interview technique, would count against me. I attended two interviews and received two no-thank-you letters.

Three weeks after the unveiling of Johnny Ach's memorial, Sandy knocked on the door of my room and told me to accompany him to the King's Arms in Kyleakin. He had a proposition. I hadn't seen Sandy for a while – he had a habit of disappearing for weeks at a time and never telling where he'd been or what he'd been up to.

We sat at a table in the saloon of the pub and I began maundering on about 'the end'. Sandy pecked at his pint, suffering my whingeing with stoical indifference.

'I've heard,' he said, once I'd finally let it all out. 'What are you going to do?'

'I don't know.'

'Well, where are you going to go if you leave here?'

'I don't know,' I said and looked away out of the window. 'It's the end.'

'No it isn't,' he said. 'I've got a job for you.'

I wondered if he was going to ask me to help renovate *Ebb 'n Flow*. But winter was coming. We wouldn't get much done under all that rain.

'Have you ever seen a mussel farm?' Sandy said.

I sipped my pint, shook my head.

Sandy had 'a good friend', Dougie, who owned one on Skye and had some work going.

'It'll be a doddle,' Sandy said. 'There's about a month's work there at least. And I'm sure Dougie'll have other work for you after.' He wrote down a telephone number. 'You can borrow one of my cars.' (Sandy had several – all of them wrecks.)

As we drank on I painted a picture in my mind of myself as a tough roustabout character – all sea boots and stout waterproof trousers, out in all weathers, bashing through storms. I would become a Local, working along-side and accepted – respected even – by the Natives. I'd nestle into community life, make a real *go* of it, find myself a serene Highland lass, raise a family, stay forever.

As the rain-soaked afternoon drew on and the pub filled and the noise levels grew, as we sat staring through rain-spattered windows to the bridge and the island and Kyle opposite, after several pints of beer and numerous pipe dreams, Sandy let out a long sigh and said, 'Folk come to Skye to let the rain wash away the past.' He didn't expand on this, just followed it up with a gentle nudge of his elbow and a waggle of his pint glass to remind me it was my turn to get the drinks in. I knew Sandy well enough by now to know he wasn't about to let on what it was in his past he'd come to have washed away, so I pushed back my chair, pushed past the few shy tourists standing beside the merry-go-round fruit machine, past the rowdy Local lads crowding and crowing round the pool table, shimmied between the Natives on stools hogging the bar and stepped up, where the jovial, pink-cheeked barmaid spotted me, brightened further and came over to ask what it was I'd be wanting in the way of a drink.

I phoned Dougie quite late the following morning.

'Aye well, we offered the job to Sandy but when we hadn't heard from him . . . Can you come over tomorrow and I'll give you a try-out?'

I lasted two days.

The first was sunny and still. Dougie and his mate and I motored in a flat-bottomed aluminium work-boat to a processing platform moored in the middle of a bay. Using a winch, I and the other man (who never told me his name and was probably right not to bother) hauled up strings which had hundreds of mussels grown large clinging to them. We manoeuvred the strings over a hopper and with gloved hands stripped them of their crop. The mussels fell into the hopper, where they were hosed, washed and conveyed through a riddle and grader into string sacks. Once we'd harvested all the strings in one area of the loch, we weighed anchor and moved the platform along to the next batch of strings. We did this all day. *Factory work*, I said to myself. *Repetitive, but not back-breaking. I can do this.*

I ended the first day full of confidence and renewed hope.

The next day Dougie told me he had a different job for me, the job he'd told Sandy about. I stepped into the work-boat and we motored out to a tired-looking wooden fishing boat, twenty feet long, fat and heavy, bobbing on a buoy. We climbed aboard. The wheelhouse, a tiny cabin forward, an inboard engine and a winch, had all seen better days. I kept out of the way while Dougie fiddled with the engine which, after a few coughs, chugged into life. Dougie aimed the fishing boat for one of the long lines of grey floats – like water butts lying on their side connected by lengths of rope – that lay in the loch. When we reached the floats, Dougie stuck the engine in neutral, leant over the side of the boat and knotted a short length of cord from the boat to the line of floats. Once the boat was secured he cut the engine and passed out some old waterproofs and thick rubber gloves.

'You'll be wanting these,' he said. 'It's a muddy job.'

Silence overwhelmed us.

'Now,' said Dougie. 'So you tie the boat to the line in the water with the cord like I've done, then you lower that hook through the winch and attach it to the line.'

It was a blue-sky day. A slight breeze was blowing onto the boat, easing it away from the line of floats.

'Once you've got the hook on the line, you can haul it up with the winch using these controls . . .' He touched a lever with a knob on the end beside the winch, and the line we were moored to rose into the air and was pulled towards the boat, '. . . but watch your fingers in the winch there. It'll take your hand off.'

Once the line was suspended above the water, I could see that between every one of the floats there were eight coils of string hanging from the line. Each of these string coils had plastic pegs attached at intervals along its length and a weight on the end. Tiny baby mussels clung to the pegs and the string. The coils had been tied up with a finer piece of string.

'Then you take this knife . . .' Dougie pulled a blade from a sheath screwed onto the boat beside the winch, '. . . reach over the side of the boat and cut the wee string binding the coils so the line of babies hangs straight down in the water. Like you saw yesterday, once the mussels have grown full size we haul them up and harvest them.

'Then you reverse the winching, take the hook off the line, untie the cord, pull the boat along to the next bit of the line, tie her on with the cord, attach the hook, winch the line up, cut the string off the coil, release the babies, and on you go again. We'll see how many you can manage.'

Dougie's mate had looked on silently all this time. I glanced up at him, hoping for some sign of encouragement. I didn't even register acknowledgment.

After asking if I had sandwiches and a flask, Dougie and his mate climbed down into the aluminium work-boat and sped across the bay to the processing platform and started up the hopper.

To begin with I was enthusiastic, as I nearly always am when presented with a new challenge. *I'll show those boys,* I told myself, *I'll win them over and they'll slap me on the back at the end of the week and tell me they never thought the skinny south-erner had it in him.*

I got the hang of the job and kept an eye on my fingers, the winch, the ropes and the knife and worked hard and fast for four hours. I broke for lunch and sat in the sun and all that blue; felt the ache in my shoulders of real work, and it felt good. *And at the pub at Isleornsay we'll buy drinks and we'll talk and laugh like workmates do and I will* know *I've been accepted and I'll stay and make a life among you fine people.*

Then the wind picked up and the work became punishing. I struggled on, bending over the high gunwales to haul the boat along while the wind hit it broadside on and pushed it away from the lines and the floats. The wind was too strong and the boat too heavy. For me. At about 3 p.m. my back and shoulders gave out. The last coil of baby mussels sank below the surface. I sat down at the stern of the boat.

Dougie had told me that if I got into trouble I was to phone him on his mobile. I tried him, but out there in the loch there was no signal. I stood and waved my arms at the men on the processing platform. Dougie and his mate carried on working. I couldn't tell if they'd seen me or not, they were so far away.

'I give up,' I said, mostly to myself but perhaps to everything. 'I give up,' and felt wretched.

After some time the men motored across to me and Dougie came aboard.

'There's a crosswind, aye?' He started the inboard and made for the mooring buoy at the end of the loch. We moored the boat, tidied up, and transferred to the work-boat.

I said: 'I'm not physically strong enough.'

'Aye.'

We thrummed across the loch. I sat in the front of the boat, out of the way. Dougie and his mate had turned themselves away from me and I noticed for the first time, as I sat hoping for some kind of sympathy, some acknow-ledgement, from those thrawn Highlanders, how so very broad their backs were.

I coaxed Sandy's car back to Kyleakin and drove round to the Bright Water Visitors' Centre. The trustee who man-aged the Centre was sitting in front of a computer screen in the office at the back of the building. I told her I would be leaving the island in a week's time. She didn't say much. She knew my circumstances.

'We'll be sorry to see you go,' she said finally. It was

what they all said: 'We'll be sorry to see you go and your work here will be remembered.'

During my last week on the island an abnormally high spring tide, the fallout from a strong equinoctial gale in the Outer Hebrides, lifted my dinghy from where I'd hauled it high up the slipway, ripped it from its rope tethers, dashed it against the rocks and dragged it down the slip into the bay. It was holed, terminally, fore and aft.

A few days later, Sandy and I sailed *Emma Gaze* to a boatyard in Broadford, where the old yawl was to spend the winter hauled out on the hard. Sandy had persuaded a woman who sang in the local Gaelic choir to come along with us. It was a rum day for a sail – cold, the wind blowing hardly at all. The rain fell softly, dotting the sea around us. We ghosted along with all sails set, hunched up together in the cockpit, the choir lady singing Gaelic laments in the rain. Once *Emma Gaze* was out of the water, Sandy and I unstepped the mast. Without it the yawl seemed tiny and forlorn, and looking at her it hardly seemed possible that something so small and so derelict could have given us all so much joy.

I packed up my things. There wasn't much. I lost a game of chess with Marcus in my room, out of the rain, before he quietly shook my hand with both of his and rushed off to catch his bus back to Broadford. I spent a day saying my goodbyes to Pete, John, the trustees – strangers who had become my friends. I couldn't trust myself to say too much or prolong these meetings, there was a tightness in my throat that made me sound funny and my eyes, betraying me, kept leaking. The look of one particular face, watching me through a rain-smeared window as I skulked away, haunts me still.

Most places, as soon as I've arrived, I'm plotting my escape. A growing familiarity with somewhere, and with its people, leads to boredom and restlessness. There is a big, wide-open world out there and there are many paths to follow to see where they lead. Leaving is usually so easy for me.

I have never felt so distressed about leaving a place and its people in my life.

≈

'I've been living up here for years but this is the first time I've been down to Sandaig,' Sandy says as we pull up beside the gate.

'Yeah, but you're not interested, are you,' I say as we get down from his van.

'Not really,' says Sandy. 'Someone gave me the book once,' and I wonder: *Which one, Sandy! He wrote eleven.* 'She was a Maxwell fan. But I never got around to reading it.'

He looks around, slams the driver's-side door. 'It's on *Ebb 'n Flow* somewhere. I think so, anyway . . . though I've not seen it for a while. Maybe I gave it away.'

I haven't been down to Sandaig for months, not since

my car conked out. You really need a car or a boat to get to Sandaig.

'Otters, though,' Sandy sniffs in the crisp damp air, 'I've got a lot of time for otters. My dog likes them too. But they look . . . untrustworthy somehow. I wouldn't want one as a pet.'

We hop over the gate and tramp along the rutted and lorry-slurried track through the fir plantation. The sharp tang of pine spices the air. We pass piles of newly cut, sap-oozing logs. I've seen stacks of these logs on Kyle Quay, awaiting trans-shipment to Norway. It seems crazy, symptomatic of the madness of the modern world – shipping Norwegian Spruce to Norway, the twenty-first-century equivalent of carrying coals to Newcastle.

The track forks. A cairn marks the footpath down to Sandaig. Sandy and I duck under fir trees that have fallen across the path, and splash through muddy puddles. The burn clamours in the ravine below us. We reach the lower level of the hillside where the plantation is still thick, the floor a carpet of dropped pine needles, and through a gap in the trees I can see the islands and the sea meadow below.

'Isleornsay!' Sandy says, and points to the lighthouse and the white houses a mile away across the Sound of Sleat. I can see the burn rushing silver, flowing through the avenue of alders to the sea. 'The ring of bright water,' I say.

We walk on down, balance our way across the rope

bridge and pad through wet grass to Edal's cairn. All traces of the rowan tree, just like the house, are gone now. The nearby larch has grown tall and full.

'Who puts all these shells and stones and flowers here?'

'Fans.'

'Why?' Sandy says, amazed. 'What's the point?'

'There's always more for Edal than for Maxwell,' I say and lead Sandy across the meadow to Maxwell's grave.

'*Gavin Maxwell, born 15th July 1914, died 7th September 1969*,' Sandy reads. 'He was born on Saint Swithin's Day. So he was what . . . fifty-five when he died. I'm ol— . . . he was still *young*.'

'Cancer,' I say. 'The primary was in his lungs but by the time it was diagnosed it was everywhere, his skull, his femur, his back . . .'

He died as the charred remains of the house were being bulldozed into the dunes.

'Grab life when you can, Dan,' Sandy says. 'I've known too many people who've said, "When I retire I'm going to . . ." or "Just a few more years doing this, just till we're set up and then . . ." and then something like that comes and takes them away.'

It is a still, dull mid-November day. I have visited Sandaig so many times over the years, in all weathers, and so often alone. Dara and I had been boys when we'd camped down here so long ago. Now I am going grey and I haven't seen Dara in twenty years.

'That's Raef's croft,' I say, pointing.

We walk over to it. 'I tried to rent it once.'

No one knows for sure what caused the inferno that gutted the house at Sandaig. Sparks from a dying fire? Faulty electrics? An incautiously dropped cigarette? No one knows.

'Nice little place,' Sandy says. 'It looks knackered though. Like the estate want it to fall down.'

'I think they do,' I say. 'I think they're fed up with Maxwell fans coming down here traipsing all over their land.'

The driving Highland rain is quickly demolishing the building. The guttering has collapsed and hangs over the shuttered doorway like a furrowed brow. Mould and algae have stained the once white walls a dirty grey and green. There are no longer wooden fish boxes stacked neatly under tarpaulin awaiting Raef's return, no tap tied to the fence with its black plastic pipe leading back to the burn. The telegraph and electricity poles are still there, but the wires are disconnected and hang uselessly in the air. The meadow in front of the croft is a squelchy, boggy mess. The beaches are littered with plastic bottles, crisp packets, lengths of nylon rope and netting, plastic bags, food packaging of all kinds, old tyres; globally available crap. Where once almost everything was biodegradable nowadays almost nothing is.

'The first few times I came here, there was an old barn behind that fence,' I say. 'Now you'd never know. It was

only sixteen years after Maxwell's death, that first time.
It seemed a long time to me then, sixteen years, but now I
know it was nothing. Sixteen years isn't very long at all.'

'Long enough to put lines on a face.' Sandy leaves me
to poke around in the roofless shed beside the croft. When
he comes out he says: 'This whole area has changed loads.
My parents used to bring me and my brother up to the
West Highlands every summer when we were kids. There
were loads of tourists even back then, and caravanners
clogging the roads. Not so many English living up here
though, people tell me. Highland culture was still strong, it
still . . . held together. It was a different place to what it has
become.'

'Better,' I say.

'No. Life was much harder. Everything took longer. It's
no better or worse up here than anywhere else you might
end up. And as for being "remote", an elderly Luisach was
asked by an English reporter once what it felt like, living
in such a remote place. "Remote?!" booms the Lewisman.
"Remote from where?"'

'I'd like to have lived up here back in the black-and-
white days,' I say, and Sandy laughs.

'You've admitted defeat in these days of colour, when
life here is so *easy*. If you can't hack it now, how long would
you have lasted back then?'

He sniffs. 'I spoke with your Jimmy Watt once.'

He is an enigma, Sandy.

'I had a load of Ballachulish slates I wanted to sell that had come off a house somewhere. I put an advert in the *Free Press* and Jimmy Watt phoned. He's a bit of a lady-killer, I hear. Anyway, we haggled for a while but couldn't agree on a price. I managed to get shot of them in the end to an English bloke on one of those renovation projects. And I was in the Glenelg Inn once with a mate who pointed out Terry Nutkins sitting in a corner with his wife. I'd been wondering what that bloke off *Animal Magic* was doing up here.'

'Oh yeah, right,' I say, 'and I suppose you also had that Kathleen Raine in the back of your taxi once.'

'Who? What? I've never driven a taxi.'

'Kathleen Raine. She was a poet. She . . . oh never mind. It doesn't matter any more.'

'Oh. All right. Anyway, and I used to drink with Tex Geddes in the Broadford Hotel. We had some wild sessions in there when he was alive, I tell you. Hell of a character. He told me a few stories . . . about your Maxwell.'

I take Sandy on a tour of the rest of Sandaig. We walk along the burn and I show him the outcrop of rock with the grassy top and parapet where I used to pitch my tent out of the way of the cattle and the midges. I show him the remains of the old boat on the beach, the sand martin burrows in the cliffs by the mouth of the burn, and the rope swing beneath the natural arch in the cliffs along the shore. The tide is in and the flat sea pushes up against the land, cutting us off from the string of islands and their white seashell beaches and rabbit-cropped swards. The Northern Lighthouse Board has replaced the Lilliputian lighthouse (which now stands above the slipway of the Kylerhea–Glenelg Ferry) with an ugly, modern, boxy beacon. We see few birds, and no ravens. We come across some droppings, but they are of fox, not otter or wildcat. The Sound of Sleat is empty of boats and Sandaig is an empty, haunted stage. There is little life down here now. The players left a long time ago and will never return.

Gavin Maxwell, were he alive today, would be over a hundred years old. Raef Payne and Richard Frere and Tex Geddes have passed on. Kathleen Raine died in 2003 at the age of ninety-five, run into by a reversing car on Paultons Square, where she had moved to a house near the one she had once shared with Maxwell. The older generation of Glenelg and the surrounding villages still retain memories of the odd, highly strung, spendthrift 'otter man', but they are hazy memories now, mired by the mists of time. Soon no one who knew Maxwell or the house and menagerie at Sandaig will remain.

I show Sandy the waterfall. He yawns and says: 'Rather a gloomy spot, though it must have been brighter when there weren't all these blooming fir trees crowding out the light.'

The weather begins to turn. Grey clouds are building and merging, darkening the air above us. We jump over the puddles that spread out under the gate by the croft and begin the steep walk up the Land Rover track.

'I've never really understood your interest in Gavin Maxwell,' Sandy says.

I have never been completely sure myself, but by now I have worked it out and so I tell him.

It wasn't about the otters, although the keeping of wild animals as pets is something I share with Maxwell, part of my own unconventional family history; it was about something else.

Literature can be a very intimate art form. The act of reading a book is a silent meeting of minds, and sometimes a bond – a very powerful but always one-sided bond – takes place. Such a meeting is filled with artifice and impossibility. As a teenager, I imagined I had met Gavin Maxwell in his books. I fell in love with the idea of the kind of life that he and the boys lived, and with the pictures he painted in my mind. I connected, and I was seduced. But what I connected with so strongly was a carefully constructed version of himself. Compelling, but also quite false. Because part of his genius was to create a semblance of honesty in his books, enchanting and involving the reader by telling us all about it. He made us feel like we were his *intimates*. It was all a mirage in the end, of course, just *Art*, but Gavin Maxwell introduced me to the Highlands and the Hebrides, and he showed me the power of the written word. And in my imaginings of Gavin Maxwell – who'd taught me things and taken me on adventures – I found the surrogate father that, all along, subconsciously, I'd been searching for.

I was a shy, bookish, country-bred boy, living among others whose interests I did not share, and I possessed the credulousness and innocence of all country-bred children. And I am a dreamer. But dreams aren't sustainable, and they're never as good in reality as they are in your head. All my life I have been led on by writers whose words on a page I have fallen in love with. We think of books as tablets of stone, but all writing, even the autobiographical, is full of fiction: a fraudulent, transmuted reality; a distorted projection of truth. I got lost early on.

At the top of the Land Rover track, by the parking place that looks down over the domain, over the croft and the islands, Sandy and I stop to catch our breaths.

'They're prisons,' Sandy says, 'places like that. Cut off from the road, the only useful access from the sea, no neighbours for miles around. They're all right for the occasional retreat, to get away from the world, but to try and live in them full-time! A prison, like your island must have been for those lighthouse keepers and their families. And there's something trophy-home-ish about them too, somewhere for your mates to come and see and then envy you for owning such a beautiful place. And they're impractical, and expensive to run. Much like Gavin Maxwell was, I'd say – expensive to run and impractical.'

Sandy starts off up the track but I hang back, looking down on Camusfeàrna, over the domain, over the gravestones and the deserted stage, its dramas all played out.

The books were so full of incident, and life. Now there is nothing, just loneliness, an emptiness blown by the wind.

I hear Sandy stop, walk back to where I am standing. He touches my arm.

'Come on, Dan,' he says. 'Come away.'

I turn away from Camusfeàrna, look at Sandy. He is contemplating the sky.

'You know, Dan, it's better not to have heroes. But if you *have*, don't get too close. Because if you do, you'll only find they've got feet of clay, just like the rest of us.

'And,' he says, 'I think, God help us, yet again, it's going to rain.'

We set off along the track and I ask who Saint Swithin was and Sandy tells me about the saint and about other things as we press on through the pines up to the road and his van. Then we drive down the mountain to Glenelg and away home, whatever that is and wherever it turns out to be.

A Clarification

The real name of Kyleakin Lighthouse Island is Eilean
Bàn. The trust that manages the island and the Bright
Water Visitors' Centre is called the Eilean Bàn Trust.
However, Eilean Bàn is not the island's original 'given'
name, which is in fact Eilean nan Gillean. Due to a cartog-
rapher's error way back in the mists of time (1872), the
lighthouse island became misnamed. In Gaelic, eilean
means 'island', bàn means 'white', and gillean means
'boys' or 'youth' (although gillean may be a corruption of
gilean, which means 'clefts' or 'gullies'). I have called the
place I lived on and write about here Kyleakin Lighthouse
Island, because I prefer that name and because it is what
Gavin Maxwell called it.

I have not always used people's real names in *Island of
Dreams*. I have omitted people who were there, and the
timeframe of my sojourn on the island has been rearranged. This has been done less from a need to obscure
than from the needs of the memoir form, and *story*.

Acknowledgements

Thanks are due to Suzanne Arnold and past, present and future trustees of the Eilean Bàn Trust for letting me onto the island in the first place, and for continuing to champion the life and work of Gavin Maxwell.

Book- and writing-business thanks to: Kris Doyle (for opening the door and much else besides), Sara Lloyd (for crucial intel.), Christopher Sinclair-Stevenson (for a fine eye and dash), Iain Finlayson, Peter Benson, Rupert Heath, Gillian MacKenzie & Niall Griffiths (supportive insiders), Will Atkins (for critiquing the text), Philippa McEwan (in advance), Sarah Drummond (Illustrator), Stuart Wilson (for the cover design), Hemesh Alles (Map maker), Claire Gatzen, Dina Obolsky, Mindy Chillery; Jim Taylor (for writerly missives and the first review), Peter Urpeth & the anonymous work-in-progress reader at Hi-Arts, the Academi Critical Service for Writers, Sam Hawkins, Sara Hunt & Craig Hillsley, and Bob Davidson & Moira Forsyth.

Thank you, Judy Scott (for affordable lodgings), Sally Baker, Awen Hamilton, Nia Wyn Roberts, Ceri Shore & Tŷ Newydd (for the work and the rooms), Bernie, Russ & Stefan (for percipience in Rishikesh many moons ago), and Tina (for demanding a walk at four every day).

Et enfin, thank you, Ali Roberts (my lovely).

I am grateful to the following for permission to include copyright material:

Jimmy Watt, the Marsh Agency, and Jane Frere.

The photograph of Gavin Maxwell and Edal on page 3, and of Camusfeàrna on page 287, are reproduced by kind permission of Gavin Maxwell Enterprises Ltd.

Select Bibliography

Books

MAXWELL, GAVIN, *Harpoon at a Venture*, Rupert Hart-Davis, 1952.

——, *God Protect Me from My Friends*, Longmans, 1956.

——, *A Reed Shaken by the Wind*, Longmans, 1957.

——, *The Ten Pains of Death*, Longmans, 1959.

——, *Ring of Bright Water*, Longmans, 1960.

——, *The Otters' Tale*, Longmans, 1962.

——, *The Rocks Remain*, Longmans, 1963.

——, *The House of Elrig*, Longmans, 1965.

——, *Lords of the Atlas*, Longmans, 1966.

——, *Seals of the World*, Constable, 1967.

——, *Raven Seek Thy Brother*, Longmans, 1968.

ARMEN, JEAN-CLAUDE, *Gazelle-Boy*, The Bodley Head, 1974.

BATHURST, BELLA, *The Lighthouse Stevensons*, HarperCollins, 1999.

BERNARD, PHILIPPA, *No End to Snowdrops: A Biography of Kathleen Raine*, Shepheard-Walwyn Ltd, 2009.

BOTTING, DOUGLAS, *Gavin Maxwell: A Life*, HarperCollins, 1993.

BROWN, HAMISH, *Hamish's Mountain Walk*, Paladin, 1986.

COCKER, MARK, *Loneliness and Time: British Travel Writing in the Twentieth Century*, Secker & Warburg, 1992.

COOMBS, FRANKLIN, *The Crows*, Batsford, 1978.

FITZGERALD O'CONNOR, PATRICK, *Shark-O!*, Secker & Warburg, 1953.

FRASER DARLING, FRANK, *Island Years*, G. Bell & Sons, 1940.

FRASER DARLING, FRANK & BOYD, J. MORTON, *The Highlands and Islands*, Fontana, 1972.

FRERE, RICHARD, *Maxwell's Ghost*, Gollancz, 1976.

GEDDES, TEX, *Hebridean Sharker*, Herbert Jenkins, 1960.

GLASIER, PHILIP, *As the Falcon Her Bells*, Heinemann, 1963.

HILL, PETER, *Stargazing: Memoirs of a Lighthouse Keeper*, Canongate, 2003.

HOGG, JAMES, *James Robertson-Justice: What's the Bleeding Time?*, Tomahawk Press, 2008.

HOWARD, ELIZABETH JANE, *Slipstream*, Macmillan, 2002.

HUXLEY, ELSPETH, *Peter Scott: Painter and Naturalist*, Faber & Faber, 1995.

KNIGHTON, C. S., *Kyleakin Lighthouse: A Short History*, privately printed, 1982.

LEWIS, WILLIAM JOHN, *Ceaseless Vigil: My Lonely Years in the Lighthouse Service*, Harrap, 1970.

LISTER-KAYE, JOHN, *The White Island*, Longmans, 1972.

——, *The Seeing Eye: Notes of a Highland Naturalist*, Allen Lane, 1980.

LOCKLEY, R. M., *The Island*, André Deutsch, 1969.

——, *Orielton*, André Deutsch, 1977.

LORENZ, KONRAD, *King Solomon's Ring*, Methuen & Co., 1952.

MACKENZIE, R. F., *Escape from the Classroom*, Collins, 1965.

MAITLAND, ALEXANDER, *Wilfred Thesiger: The Life of the Great Explorer*, HarperCollins, 2006.

MITCHELL, IAN, *Isles of the West*, Berlinn Ltd, 2006.

NIALL, IAN, *The New Poacher's Handbook*, Heinemann, 1960.

PACKHAM, CHRIS, *Rocky Shorelands*, Collins, 1989.

PARKER, TONY, *The Lighthouse*, Hutchinson, 1975.

PATTERSON, KEVIN, *The Water In Between: A Journey at Sea*, Viking, 2000.

PIKE, OLIVER G. TUCK, MAGDALEN F. P., *Wild Nature Wooed and Won*, Jarrold & Son, 1909.

RAINE, KATHLEEN, *The Year One: Poems*, Hamish Hamilton, 1952.

——, *On a Deserted Shore*, Hamish Hamilton, 1973.

——, *The Lion's Mouth*, Hamish Hamilton, 1977.

REED, LAURANCE, *The Soay of Our Forefathers*, Berlinn Ltd, 2002.

SCOTT, PETER, *The Eye of the Wind*, Hodder & Stoughton, 1961.

STANDHOPE, P. F., *Truth or Consequences*, Cork Street Books, 1914.

THESIGER, WILFRED, *Arabian Sands*, Longmans, 1959.

——, *The Marsh Arabs*, Longmans, 1964.

THOMSON, DAVID, *The People of the Sea*, Arena, 1990.

WATKINS, ANTHONY, *The Sea My Hunting Ground*, Heinemann, 1958.

WATSON, GRAHAM, *Book Society*, André Deutsch, 1980.

WAYRE, PHILIP, *The River People*, Collins, 1976.

——, *The Private Life of the Otter*, Collins, 1979.

WHITE, T. H., *The Goshawk*, Cape, 1951.

Television and Radio Documentaries

BBC2, *Ring of Bright Water and Beyond,* The World About Us series, 1979.

BBC Scotland, *Memories of Maxwell,* EX:S, 1999.

BBC, *Gavin Maxwell: An Elegy,* Radio Scotland, 2006.

BBC, *Terry Nutkins: In the Ring of Bright Water,* Radio 4, 2009.

Magazine Articles and Papers

HILLABY, J. & KLEBOE, RAYMOND S., 'Shark Hunting', *Picture Post,* 21 September 1946.

THESIGER, WILFRED & MAXWELL, GAVIN, 'Marsh Dwellers of Southern Iraq', *National Geographic,* February 1958.

DICKINS, ANTHONY, 'Gavin Maxwell: A Postscript', *London Magazine,* August/September 1976.

Inventory Acc. 10555, 'The Papers of Gavin Maxwell & Gavin Maxwell Enterprises Ltd', Manuscripts Division, National Library of Scotland, Edinburgh.